T0078388

# TWO-TIMED:

## AN ADOLESCENT CANCER MEMOIR

**DANIELLE DUCHATEAU**

author HOUSE®

AuthorHouse™
1663 Liberty Drive
Bloomington, IN 47403
www.authorhouse.com
Phone: 833-262-8899

Published by AuthorHouse   01/20/2021

ISBN: 978-1-6655-1283-1 (sc)
ISBN: 978-1-6655-1284-8 (e)

Library of Congress Control Number: 2021900347

Print information available on the last page.

*For My Family*

*My mom, Sara – thank you for crushing hundreds of pills into gel caps so I could swallow them more easily, and for staying with me through all those hard nights in the hospital*

*My dad, Paul – thank you "Nurse Paul" for doing daily line care, giving shots, and for driving us regularly to and from treatments*

*My brother, Christian – thank you for visiting every time I was inpatient, and making me laugh*

*My brother, Charlie – thank you for making the hospital closer to home by letting us stay at your house*

*My sisters-in-law, Annbritt and Melissa – thank you for your support*

*In Memory Of*
*My grandmother, Dorothy Gustafson*
*My uncle, Bob Gustafson*
*All the fallen cancer warriors I've had the privilege of knowing*

*Thank You*
*Dr. Linda Stork – who took excellent care of me, and was by my side through both treatments*
*The Children's Hospital Denver Oncology and Bone Marrow Transplant Departments*

# PREFACE

This is the story of my journey as an adolescent through two bouts with non-Hodgkin's lymphoma – as told through journals written at the time. From the beginning of my first cancer treatment through the end of my second, I kept both "everyday journals" with descriptive entries about my experiences, and "secret journals" of writings and poetry. I turned to my secret journals in emotionally difficult moments. Often told to just be positive, and reassured that everything would be all right, I didn't want anyone to know that I felt any differently. I needed a place to express my "bad" feelings, and my fears that I might not be all right. There are a couple of reasons that I decided to write this memoir, and to include *all* of the journals. After the end of treatment, I decided that since cancer was a significant part of my life story, I wanted to share it. I told everyone that I was an "open book" when it came to talking about my experiences because I wanted them to know that *people do survive cancer.* But I never shared the whole story. I thought that if I was honest about my mental and emotional struggles during treatment, and after as a survivor, the image that people had of me as being positive, strong and brave would be shattered, and the story would no longer be inspirational or provide hope. However, I realized that I would be defeating the purpose of this memoir if I left out the parts where I struggled. There is no such thing as a normal experience when facing the rigors of cancer treatment, or the challenges or survivorship, and it is important that no patient or survivor ever feels they cannot admit that they are struggling. And that is why I am *sharing the whole story*.

Most of us can bring to mind a time when we saw someone coping with a wretched situation, and thought that we would not be able to do it. One of my father's students had a child less than a year old who was diagnosed with cancer, and he told my father about this disastrous turn of events – recounting stories of unpleasant procedures, multiple surgeries, and rigorous chemotherapy treatments. My father told my mother and I over dinner one night, and we all agreed that the situation was unthinkable. About a month after that, I was diagnosed with cancer, and we found ourselves in the same position. We were told by some that the cancer was "God's plan" for me, and that whether or not I survived, it was "God's will." These platitudes made me uncomfortable then, and now as an adult, I hear them offered to countless others in varying tragic situations. Although they may be offered in the spirit of providing comfort to the aggrieved, I find them to be presumptuous and inappropriate – stemming from personal beliefs imposed upon others who may not share them. I do not believe anyone *ever* has the right to rationalize another's misfortune in this manner – especially when these comments are made to children.

When I was first diagnosed with cancer, my image of the world shifted. The invincibility that I felt entitled to as a young person was taken away. I was still a teenage girl who had the same interests and feelings as other girls my age, but my life was anything but normal. My cancer first emerged as a swollen lymph node on my fourteenth birthday, and my seventeenth birthday was marked by the first chemotherapy treatment following relapse. During a stage of life already marked by a concern over appearances, and the effects of increasing hormones, I experienced hair loss, stretch marks, hypothyroidism, and premature ovarian failure leading to menopause. As my peers were building relationships and developing a sense of identity, I felt increasingly isolated, and began to feel that my cancer was what defined me.

Just after being diagnosed the first time, at the end of seventh grade when I would have been heading off to summer music camp, something appalling happened. A couple of girls I knew from the year before called me after hearing about my diagnosis. "It's too bad you can't come to camp this year since you have cancer and you're going to die," they taunted cruelly, while laughing uncontrollably. Then they hung up. Fast forward three years. After being diagnosed for the second time, at the end of my sophomore year of high school, something amazing happened. I was part of an advanced placement program, and I had a couple close friends, but few other social connections. One of my friends circulated a card for me for students within our program to sign. To my surprise, not only did the card have many kind and encouraging messages from classmates, but attached were pages upon pages of touching notes from students outside our program whom I did not know at all. Both experiences were socially significant to me and left lasting impressions. And it was all because of cancer.

As I was about to begin treatment the first time, I needed to have my braces removed before my immune system became compromised because of the risk of infection. I had only had them for about three months, and the orthodontist refused to remove them despite the risk, but his arrogance turned out to be a blessing in disguise. I was sent to the dental clinic at the children's hospital, and a friendly young dentist talked to me the entire time the braces were being removed. She asked me why I had to be at the hospital, and when I told her I had cancer, she told me that she was a cancer survivor. She had also been through treatment as a teenager, and had been in remission for ten years…from non–Hodgkin's lymphoma. It was amazing for me to meet someone who had survived the same type of cancer, and had been around the same age. I do not think I ever saw myself as being that ray of hope to someone else. After completing my cancer treatments, I told my parents that I felt badly about going to long-term follow-up appointments because I "looked healthy and had hair." They reassured me that when we were in the waiting room during my treatments, and they saw a healthy patient come in for a long-term follow-up, it gave them hope. Long after treatments had ended, when I told people that I had been through cancer twice, they remarked that it was hard to believe because I looked so *normal*. This compliment always amused me since it seemed like they expected they would be able to pick the cancer survivor out of a lineup for not looking "normal." Often when I attend an event as a survivor, and see others who are still battling cancer – especially children and adolescents – again I feel guilty for looking "normal." Then, I remind myself of what my parents said, and try to replace that feeling with hope. I hope that when young cancer patients, or their parents see me, they can envision adult survivorship from childhood cancer.

Since the time that I went through treatment, recognition of the psychological ramifications of cancer treatment has significantly increased. A basic search on the subject yields millions of results providing reassurance to patients and their families that it is normal and acceptable to have feelings of fear, anxiety, anger or sadness following diagnosis – and to seek help if needed. Unfortunately, fewer results provide reassurance to survivors, indicating a lesser perceived need. After all, why would anyone need reassurance when they are told that they *don't* have cancer, or when they should just be thankful they survived? The need for support following the end of treatment is just as important as the need following diagnosis. The same feelings are present, if for different reasons. Fear of relapse. Anxiety over every physical ailment. Anger because your friends didn't make it. Sadness over permanent changes. And guilt. Guilt...because you have all these feelings other than just being grateful. And guilt...because you survived.

After months, or even years of cancer treatment, it is just as unrealistic to expect to emerge emotionally unscathed, as it is to expect to emerge without any long-term effects or scars. Dealing with a mix of emotions at the end of treatment, while at the same time grappling with how to reintegrate into a more conventional existence, is a daunting task. I believe such a transition is even more difficult at a young age, when there are still so many developmental changes occurring physically, mentally, and socially. When I returned to school following my treatments, I felt completely out of place mentally and socially, as if I had missed a few steps along the way, and could never catch up.

Cancer is part of my story, and being a survivor is part of my identity, but it is not my entire identity as I felt it was when I was younger. At the end of my second treatment, I decided I was going to write my story and publish it. I even thought of the perfect title for my book: *Two-Timed: An Adolescent Cancer Memoir*. I thought of it because I felt two-timed by my own body, whose very defense system had attacked itself, and it had happened to me twice. But I didn't write the story. I decided I couldn't very well write an "adolescent memoir," being well into my twenties - but I still had all of the journals I had written. Several more years elapsed – and twenty-three years after my cancer journey began – I am finally "writing" the story.

# PROLOGUE

This journal is a well-known secret - and while it pleases everyone to know I'm writing – would anyone be proud knowing this was the result of my efforts? What starts as a stream of consciousness becomes a deluge of introspection – flowing from the prison of my mind to lighten its burden. I never intend for anyone to read this – lest they be shocked and disappointed; but if it may help even one other person – any risk taken would be worth it. I've glossed over pain and fear with smiles like sealant – to keep darkness from seeping into light; but that doesn't mean it ever ceases to exist. Sleep eluded me those nights during treatment – when I thought I might never wake again; and every night since – I both long for it and dread it – because slumber isn't always peaceful. Visions of loss and death have free rein over my defenseless mind, and dislodged emotions pass from nightmares into reality. The nightmares are steeped in distorted memories, and the ghosts of each warrior who fought beside me. Sometimes I awaken smiling – thinking soon we'll be reminiscing; and others I awaken sobbing – knowing they'll always be missing. The guilt and anguish are palpable, and the perpetual thought remains: I'm dishonoring them by living, but reconciled to the fact that I must. I think of them every day – grateful to have known them – and there are glimmers of light amidst the tears as I remember them. Those who see a survivor rarely consider the cost of victory; but no war is won without losses for all – including survivors. I buried that world long ago – afraid if I shed a tear, I would never be able to stop crying again; but neither burying history, nor preventing tears from falling, kept any of the friends I lost from dying.

How much of life happens *to* you? And how much can you *control* what happens? And how much of a difference is there between them, when you consider everything – as you did when you were fourteen? Everything changed – right before everything changed. I had always been a good student, a positive role model, and a relatively happy kid; but like the flipping of a switch, I fell into a downward spiral – far more extreme than a bout of teenage angst. I spent lunch period voluntarily in detention – filling bluebooks with journals and poetry; and when writing alone wasn't sufficiently cathartic, I started cutting. One day in one of those bluebooks, I wrote "I wish I'd get cancer and die"; and two months after I wrote those seven words, I was diagnosed with non-Hodgkin's lymphoma. I'll never know if everything changed as a result of the cancer, and the differences in my body as it developed; but ironically, it saved me from myself – by threatening my life. Taken by surprise – I felt an unexpected need to fight for it. I knew cancer was only mentioned in real life when someone died from it, and that the cancer patient never survived in movies; and the correlation between my regrettable wish and subsequent diagnosis was eerie. I was told that nothing I'd done had made me sick, and that many people survived. I couldn't tell anyone that even though now I wanted to live - I was still going to die of cancer - because I'd wished it. Nothing could convince me that I'd gotten cancer by coincidence – and not by a fate I'd chosen.

We were both inpatient on the fifth floor of the hospital when C and I met, and we became comrades in battle against childhood cancer. With excited anticipation, and IV poles laden with bags of saline and chemo in tow – we'd make our way down to the activity room. We'd exchange war stories of treatment, or just play a board game together – grateful for a reprieve from constant thoughts of cancer. We were all facing our own mortality, but we were in the battle together - and despite everything, we shared moments of joy and laughter; and we played and had fun in those precious moments – just like kids without cancer. I didn't think about the unfairness that chemo and radiation were routine for us, and cancer didn't ruin watching funny movies with L – as we spent long days side by side in our beds during treatments in the outpatient infusion room; and the day an IV pole with a bag of red cells accidentally toppled in the bathroom – we laughed when the nurse said the spatter made it look like a scene from "Scream." We all knew more about pain and suffering than most adults, and we lost far too many fellow patients who had become friends; but we still had hope that even a foe as formidable as cancer could be beat.

As I look back on our experiences now - amidst fear and uncertainty - there was adaptability to recover from a setback. When I met E in a support group for young survivors years later, she reminded me of that spirit that I'd lost — because she was the embodiment of that youthful resilience. Over the course of a single hour, her deep compassion for others and sense of gratitude changed me indelibly. I remember her smile and encouragement to every single one of us — after we'd shared stories of diagnoses, treatments, and remissions; and when she was the last to speak, I remember how calmly she shared she'd relapsed just days before — after battling leukemia…for seventeen years. As she told us the devastating news of her relapse — with poise and determination to keep fighting — the thought of it being such a tragically familiar part of life for her brought me to tears. When her courageous battle ended the following year - after another relapse and complications - I felt the flame of hope had been extinguished; but I don't think E would want me to feel that way.

I try to keep myself safely within the shallows of the present, but find myself adrift in an ocean of memories — almost drowning. I turn back — each time, a little more defeated than the last; but this time, I continue. With a book of old journals, as a guide — I unfold its map of faded memories - and chart a different course than ever before. Though the book seems outdated, and the memories too faint — tears sting my eyes, unexpectedly. The journals are those of a girl I once knew — who had cancer and wrote about her experiences. She wanted to share her story, in a way that would have helped her: in a book about having cancer as a teen – written by a teen who experienced it. As I read her story, the memories become clearer. I feel what she felt, even when it's unwritten. She wasn't lost in battle, but she's been gone a long time; and I haven't been able to forget her, or let her go. The ideal she represents in my mind is the best version of myself I can remember; but now I can let her go, so I can be who I am – instead of trying to become her.

As I awaken, the fragments are pieced together – and all the memories are brought to light. While the sadness most carry feels unbearable, it is tempered with the bittersweet joy of others; and in spite of myself, I find I can smile through the tears. The story seems unfamiliar, and yet I know it by heart. It feels like yesterday, but seems like a lifetime ago. It's the story I never wrote – because it was already written; and at the heart of it is my journey with cancer: a muse, a curse, and a blessing. I've read the book before, but I never closed the first chapter: a book of journals – written by a girl who had cancer.

*I woke up in a hospital room — and not the recovery area they showed me before the surgery — where my parents would be waiting after. There was so much noise, and people walking by, in the hall I could see through the sliding glass door. I was confused by my surroundings, and thought maybe the surgery hadn't happened yet. Then I felt a sharp pain in my neck — where the swollen lymph nodes were — but a gauze dressing was there instead. I expected that pain, but there was pain and tightness in my chest too — and I did not know why. I gently touched the area, and was surprised to feel something round and hard — under another thin dressing. Then I was horrified because I realized it was held tightly in place by a neat line of stitches — closing the skin over the incision that was made to insert it. I saw my parents standing outside the room with my doctor — talking with other people I did not know — and people were constantly going in and out of the room. Everyone says I should not be scared of having cancer, and everything is going to be fine — because I am going to get better. The round plastic thing in my chest is called a port — and the surgeon placed it when the biopsy showed it was cancer — so I can start my treatment at the children's hospital right away.*

# CANCER JOURNAL INSCRIPTION

This is a note to whomever may find it – if I have lost the battle with cancer – and I am no longer there with you. I want you to be comforted – as it has been a constant struggle for me – and death is much more peaceful. Please try to understand this. I need not be remembered much, as I did not accomplish much. I hope to be thought of every so often though. Thank you for reading this, my final farewell. – Love, Danielle

## Wednesday, June 25, 1997

Well, today was my first day of treatment for the lymphoma. It is T-Cell, B-Cell and myeloid lymphoma – previously thought to be Hodgkin's Disease. The good side of this revelation is that this kind of cancer is easier to treat. The one difference – one of many – is that this disease must be treated quicker and longer. It is going to be about eleven months of difficult and trying times. At times, it is very hard for me to be confident that I will be cured someday. Many people have assured me of recovery, and told me stories of people who have been cured, but I need to see healing to be a bit more confident. The doctors seem very confident so I always try to stay positive. The activities of today were all quite exciting. I started out at 9:00 this morning with a spinal tap. Emla cream – which is numbing cream – really aided in this. They also gave me some pain reliever and some "sleepy" medicine. I was not expected to remember anything, but I can remember every single thing that happened! One of the other painful things that happened today was the removal of the braces. I was hardly sure that the people who did the procedure knew what to do. They did not bother to do anything beforehand – they just took the bracket "yanker" and pulled them out! Well, I must go to bed now. It is late and I am very tired. The last addition to the day was the pills. There were 24 pills in all today! I had nine antibiotic ones, my chemotherapy pills, and they also have me on some stomach acid control pills. Well, bye for now! I will write about tomorrow.

## Thursday, July 3, 1997

I did not write as I would have wished to sooner. The truth is that I have felt quite cruddy. The last days at the hospital (Thursday, Friday and Saturday) were not so nice. I arrived home on Sunday and was not feeling so great. Monday is the worst day that I have had – and hope I will ever have in the whole treatment. It was difficult to make myself believe that I would make it any further in the struggle. I was unable to keep any liquids down, let alone food. It was pretty serious, so we gave the doctors a call, and they decided that maybe I was stopped up. So, to make matters even worse, they had me eat prunes, and drink some juice. It was quite sickening, and my stomach had the same reaction as to anything else. To make matters more confusing, the homecare nurse showed up to instruct us on giving shots. I was feeling awful, and she had the privilege of seeing the prune juice come back up. When she learned that the hospital had already fully educated us on the subject, she became very flustered, and called her boss. A family is only allowed a certain number of visits by a nurse, so we decided that we may need it more at another time. She quickly left, and apologized for intruding upon us. We had put the Emla cream on, so we needed to do the shot while it was still numb. I believe in my state, the smallest of things could have set me off, and the shot surely did. My dad stuck it in, and I instantly started sobbing. I could tell that he was worried, and quickly assured him that it was not the shot, but just how awful I felt. My parents understood that. Now, they told me that there would be good days and bad days. Well, the next day was better. I was not feeling so great in the morning though. I took a shower, for I was feeling quite smelly after five days in a hospital bed. That is the most nightmarish shower I have ever taken! I was fine until it was time to wash my hair. Moving my head around brought every bad feeling back to me. I just stayed in long enough to wash the shampoo out, and then I came out shivering, crying, and nearly throwing up. I just stayed in my room then. It took awhile to recover from the nausea, but I later was able to eat my first real food. My first food was a baked potato from Wendy's. The steroid that I am taking started having its effect. One of the things that it does is give one a huge appetite. I haven't stopped eating since Tuesday. I am always craving something! Anyway,

I had a small treatment and some blood work done on Tuesday. My counts were still fine then, and are still up today. They will surely go down any time now, but I am thankful that they have stayed up this long. I have had one effect from all the drugs. I am a bit fragile. I am shaky, and a bit dizzy when I walk. The Vincristine treatment gave me a numb feeling in my fingers and tongue, that is only a slight inconvenience. I went today for an L-Asparaginase shot. There are two – one in each leg. They are painful, but it is a very temporary discomfort. They only took a bit of blood from my finger, and my counts are still fabulous. I believe I can truly enjoy the holiday tomorrow. Write as soon as I can!

## Wednesday, July 9, 1997

I have not written in awhile, I know, but there does not ever seem to be a right time to write. I have either been feeling badly, or we are rushing off to an appointment in Denver. We went to Denver yesterday for a treatment, and have been going pretty normally, twice a week for counts. I received the Vincristine and the Methotrexate yesterday. That is a spinal tap and an injection into the port. The spinal tap went incredibly well, and as always, the port did not bother me. I was feeling pretty good after the appointment, so we went and had a quick lunch between Subway and Wendy's, and then returned home. I was hungry, so I made some soup. I had an immediate awful, nauseous feeling. I don't know what happened. We finished watching Ivanhoe, and then we had dinner. I had noticed earlier that just walking was a strenuous effort, and it was getting a bit worse. Mother called to let the hospital know, and they said to go to the PVH emergency room, just to do some tests. Well, we were at the hospital all night doing tests, and I was on oxygen. Not a pleasant experience! We were admitted to a room by 5:00 in the morning, and we were exhausted! That was just one of many excitements of the whole thing, I guess. That is all I can say about that.

## Saturday, July 12, 1997

Well, I have not been too faithful in writing, but a lot has been going on. We went down to Denver yesterday for L-Asparaginase treatments. We returned to the hair place in the square today. My hair is very rapidly falling out now, but I am not too upset. The wig that they ordered is just wonderful! It is almost my hair color, and it even has some curl to it! Well, I think I will go rest now. Maybe more later.

## Sunday, August 29, 1997

My it has been a long time since I last wrote! Treatments are going well, as usual. I am on an extremely high dose of Prednisone. 270 mg a day! It is only for a week, thank goodness. I did many things today – everything from a walk to cello practice to piano practice. I am quite proud of myself! Well, I'll try to be better about writing!

## Friday, September 19, 1997

It has been awhile since I have written, I know. Things just get so busy, and I forget to write! I have had one or two hospital stays since the last time I wrote. I had to get my methotrexate, that has now become a monthly drug. We have made it to the last page of my treatment now, and that page will just keep repeating itself. I was supposed to have a treatment of ARA-C and VP16 this week, but my counts were too low. We are checking into the food sensitivity testing now. I went to have some blood drawn at the lab today. Thank goodness, Mr. Dopey was not there. It was the nice woman, and she kept talking to me. They have come to know me as a regular customer there. Well, I must get back to my studying now. It has been very hard to keep up my schooling with the chemo!

## The Enemy Within

There is a force within me
That quickly multiplies;
And causes pain and trouble
Of unimaginable size.
Tiny cells that once were normal
Began to become corrupt;
They invaded my once healthy system,
And my stress level went up.
The poison given to kill them,
These enemy cancer cells,
Kills everything, even healthy,
And can make life seem like hell.
The longest days of torture,
Experienced in Oncology 4A,
Are filled with sickness and headaches,
And seem longer than a day.
The hospital stays are harder,
And sometimes it is more difficult to cope.
After a devastating treatment,
It seems impossible to find any hope.
Following the treatment comes the pills,
And all counts drop within the blood.
There goes the immune system and social life,
And emotions plummet with a thud.
Depression, anxiety, or fear,
Or sometimes all three of the above;
Emotions difficult to share,
Even with those one loves.
The fearsome questions that nag,

*Will I live, will I die, is there a cure?*
*Although there is always hope,*
*Nobody can ever be sure.*
*Then there is the hair loss,*
*With nothing left to brush;*
*It sometimes breaks the heart,*
*And the sobs are hard to hush.*
*The IVs, tubes and needles,*
*Are pains that I can take.*
*The way the drugs make me feel*
*Is what I truly hate.*
*The feeling of no energy*
*And aches from meds I take;*
*The feeling I will never feel good again,*
*And that my life may be at stake.*
*So this is what the force within me*
*Has the power to do;*
*It could have been growing for months,*
*Before anyone ever knew.*
*My own body betrayed me,*
*And now there's a civil war;*
*A war that is fought within,*
*As I experience nothing like I've known before.*
*Sometimes prognoses are bad,*
*But mine is seemingly good.*
*I try to hope for the best,*
*Which anyone in this situation should.*
*This is a life I never knew,*
*But a life I've come to know;*
*And although the times are tough,*
*I try to let my strong side show.*

## Sunday, October 26, 1997

My! It has been a long time since I last wrote. Chemo is going as well as it could be. I am into the maintenance phase now, which is the last page of treatments. It is a six week cycle that I just keep repeating for six times. I am about to begin the second of these six times. Each time begins with a spinal tap and a big bunch of pills, which is not too fun. The "big bunch of pills" is the Prednisone, which I hate with a passion! Also, the TG-6 – which consists of 11 ½ pills every night for four consecutive nights. The new diet has eliminated a lot of foods I would like to have. This causes some tension. We are finding foods I can enjoy though. I have to take a lot of nutritional supplements! I feel good today. Just tired, as I usually am. I promise to write again tomorrow!

## Monday, October 27, 1997

I am very tired, so I will not write long. The day was fairly busy. My counts from the lab were completely acceptable, so I have treatment tomorrow. I went to get the wig cut today. It is much more manageable now. Well, I must go to bed now. Good night.

## Wednesday, December 31, 1997

It has been such a long time since I last wrote, and so many thoughts have gone unrecorded. I am physically feeling quite good lately, but there is almost always some sensation of being tired. That is not too surprising I suppose, considering what my body is experiencing. It is a long time when I think about the treatment, and every time I believe that I am almost halfway there, it seems like the time gets extended! I have overcome most of my thinking and fear of death, but then I hear that another soul in the support forum has passed on. I know that I am in no true danger now, but that news would bother anyone. Well, that is enough thinking for now!

*Wish*

*I wish that I could feel well,*
*And have a regular life;*
*But the illness has made me stronger,*
*And able to survive through strife.*
*I wish that I could tell them,*
*All the things that I have seen;*
*The knowledge and sense I have gained,*
*From being ill at the age of fourteen.*
*I have so much more to see,*
*And so much more to live.*
*I have so much more to love,*
*And so much more to give.*
*The illness should not end my life,*
*If it does not have to be.*
*They say I choose my own happiness,*
*And that it's all in how I see.*

## Wednesday, January 7, 1998

It was fun to have the holidays for a short while. I know that a new year marks my being ever closer to the end of treatment. I did not have my scheduled treatment yesterday, because my platelets are too low. It will probably be next week instead. I had to start drinking two vegetable drinks a day instead of one today. It is really a pain! I have been taking a nap every day, so there will probably be one this afternoon.

## Thursday, February 5, 1998

Prednisone started on Tuesday, after a treatment of Adriamycin and Vincristine. It is a very high dose of 300 mg a day this time! I do not feel too good because of that. My next treatment is just an IV push of Vincristine next Tuesday. It is not a thing that I particularly anticipate, because I do not even have to pass counts to get that treatment! The doctor was talking about my risk for osteoporosis yesterday. That gives me all the more reason to drink soy milk, because it has calcium. I actually do not feel too feminine this year. I mean, think about it! No hair, no period, thinning eyelashes. It bothers me sometimes.

## Sunday, June 14, 1998

Sometimes I feel that people do not understand how catastrophically the drugs affect me. For instance, everybody pokes fun at the irritability Prednisone causes in me, but it is really no laughing matter. It is difficult to have a sense of humor about jokes related to the effects of the drugs. Nobody has been sick, and had to have so many drugs, and none of them know how fragile and depressed cancer treatment makes me feel. Everyone jokes that I am "grumpy" when I am actually feeling like ending it, and those thoughts are never shared with anyone. I said I was proud because I thought I lost some of the extra weight after the heavy duty Prednisone last time, and they joked that my ass looked just as big as before. I just made it to the bathroom before I burst into tears and cut again after all this time. Everyone always says I am too sensitive so I try to take it all lightheartedly. There is nothing that I can do except go along and pretend like everything is great, which I do best (though not as good as I used to).

*Untitled*

*I thought about your sharpness,*
*Cutting through my pain;*
*I remembered your numbing effect,*
*And the way life feels insane.*
*Symbol of my weakness –*
*An expression of my anger;*
*A hidden expression of sadness,*
*And a moment of flirting with danger.*
*I feel you tearing at my senses,*
*And putting the pain outside.*
*I feel relief and guilt and wonder*
*Each time that you glide –*
*Across my skin,*
*Through my mind,*
*And this is why I lied.*

## Thursday, October 8, 1998

It is amazing that I have not written for months! This time has gone so quickly, and yet so slowly. It has been a tough year, but I feel that the experience has made me a better person. I have more feelings and compassion for those with serious illnesses, where before I most likely would have been like anyone else – thinking that these people with no hair and/or mental problems were weird – or in the case of those with no hair – "punk". I can not believe what I used to be like! Tomorrow, I go to my last hospital stay. It will be both joyful and sad. I hope that I do not become emotional at discharge time! I call the hospital "Hotel Torture", and the last two cancer treatments "The Cancer Diet" because I lose weight. Usually about ten pounds! Everything that has happened in the past year and a third will soon be a memory. I think I like it that way. Got to get to that hospital early and tackle that last stay!

## The Silence Unknown

*The voice within is silent,*
*Yet it has so much to say.*
*The thoughts remain unexpressed,*
*As a facade covers every day.*
*Nobody knows the pain,*
*Or damage of every thought.*
*The need to always pretend –*
*A lesson too well taught.*
*The feelings remain undiscussed,*
*As the mood swings often do too.*
*There is little peace in the silence,*
*But no more in staying true.*
*The silence is unknown,*
*As no one feels able to share,*
*The explosion of thoughts and feelings,*
*That is almost always there.*

## Friday, October 30, 1998

I deeply regret that I did not take the time to write directly after my last hospital stay. Anyway, I will try to recall how it went now. Everything went fairly smoothly, and I was really able to eat more than in previous times. Sure, there were still the hours when I felt awful and could not keep anything down. There were times when I was a pain to my mother and snapped at her. She was good to take that from me without complaint. I do not know if I could have! As embarrassing as it is to admit, something very memorable happened that last hospital stay that I will never forget. One time after I had finished my job in the bathroom, and went to flush the toilet, it stopped up! I tried to do it again, and the water just kept rising higher and higher... I decided at that point that I had better stop, or it would most certainly overflow! My mother had left the room temporarily, and I started to go into that hysterical state that I so often resort to in times of embarrassment. Not certain what to do, I called the nurse's button. She did not come. In the meantime, my mother and the cleaning lady came in. The cleaning lady did just what I dreaded – she went into the bathroom. I heard her messing with the toilet, and then it flushed! I was so relieved. By the time the nurse got to the scene of the "crime", all I said was that I called her "because my hat was full". Thank goodness for that cleaning lady! Well, now it is time to write about the most exciting news of late. Treatment is done! My last treatment was yesterday – the second day of the Ara–C/VP16 treatment. It was not as exciting a day as I had expected, I admit, but it will go down in history, literally! It will go down in history for other people because of John Glenn, and it will go down in my personal history as the day I defeated the enemy in this long war. The treatment went alright, although I did have those very sick moments when it was just awful. Sometimes I get so sick, and there is nothing to throw up, and I choke a bit. Sometimes it was uncertain to me during those times whether I would make it, or choke to death on my own saliva. I did have two scares during the treatment. Dr. K came to see me the first day, just as my mother had stepped out. She was happy to see me, for we had not met for almost six months practically! I was happy to see her, until she told me her news. She said that there had been recent studies into more effective ways of treating my cancer, and it was thought that I might benefit from receiving more chemotherapy. Another year of steroids and chemo pills to be exact. I did not know what to say. I felt like bursting into tears and screaming, "It's not fair"!, but instead I pasted a grin on my face and made a joke about being hungry again from Prednisone. Well, later she came in and said that she was sorry, and she made a mistake. This new study only affected children who did not receive spinal taps regularly. I had them continuously during treatment. I know it was a mistake, but I believe that I would have checked pretty carefully and read the fine print before I went and made a person's world turn upside down like that! The other excitement that I had during this last treatment was my reaction. During treatment, I developed a rather flushed cheek, and nobody was able to figure it out. I was given a huge dose of IV Benadryl, that really knocked me out, but fixed the problem. My leaving the clinic that last day was no big event. The only person who said goodbye was the nurse who was taking care of me. That made me a bit sad, and glad at the same time. I do not know why, but a feeling of sadness came over me when I thought of the end of treatment. I think it is a combination of missing all the kind people at Children's, and wondering if people will still care about me now. I always liked that feeling at the hospital that so many people cared for you. I will miss that. However, I am very glad to be done with chemo, and it is time to get on with a "normal" life. I know things will never be completely the same again, though.

## Wednesday, November 18, 1998

It has been a much longer time than I intended since I last wrote. There have been a few happenings in that period of time that I wish to record so that they are not forgotten. First, I had a platelet transfusion last Tuesday as my platelets were dangerously low due to the last treatment. I apparently received a rather huge bag of platelets as all the nurses were commenting on it. I had a bit of a reaction to the transfusion, itchy nose and throat, and they decided to load me up with IV Benadryl! I could not walk in a straight line for the rest of the day. The next happening was on Friday. I went to have labs to make certain that the platelets were going up. After the lab guy drew my arm, it would not stop bleeding. In a panic, assuming that my platelets had gone down, we rushed to the emergency room. They were able to stop my bleeding quickly, and said that my platelets were fine and it was the fault of the person that drew me. He must have hit the vein at the wrong angle, and torn it, making it bleed more. That episode did not help my opinion of him. Right now my red count is low, and I suffer awful headaches sometimes. I do not want to complain like everyone else though, so do not say anything. I am in one of those stages where I think our diet sucks, and doesn't help me. I have never thought it helped me. It drives me crazy sometimes! Oh well, nothing I can do.

★★★

*Saturday, December 12, 1998*
*The Christmas Letter*

*Dear Family and Friends,*

*I am very happy to inform you that I have completed my chemotherapy treatments for the cancer. My treatment lasted for almost a year and a half, and ended this past October. I want to thank all of you for your encouragement and continued support throughout this time. Without that, it would not have been possible to endure the treatment. My treatment began on June 25, 1997, just a few days after my diagnosis. The diagnosis was non-Hodgkin's T-Cell lymphoma, with a bit of B-Cell and myeloid involvement. It was decided that a year of chemotherapy treatment would be needed.*

*My treatments were at Children's Hospital in Denver. It was such a blessing to be so close to a renowned hospital such as this one. It is known as one of the top children's hospitals in the United States, and their oncology clinic follows the same treatments as many other well-known medical treatment centers. The doctors were always alert to hear of any better ways that they could treat my illness, and would inform us of any new ideas that might better the chance of a complete cure. It was also a bonus that such caring and helpful people work there. The nurses were very attentive, and would always be checking to be sure that everything was alright and that nothing was needed.*

*The chemotherapy started with a phase called the induction phase, that was five days in the hospital of intense chemotherapy. This part of treatment killed most of the cancer. After that was done, there was a phase called the consolidation phase that was* a bit milder, but still rather aggressive treatment. I went to the outpatient clinic about every other week for checkups and to get some chemotherapy. Every month during that phase there was a spinal tap, where the doctor checked my spinal fluid and injected some chemotherapy in there too. The last part of treatment was the longest, and that was the maintenance phase. This phase consisted of six cycles, each of which lasted about sixty days. The treatments were all big ones, and hard for me, but they were not as often as before. The treatments were about every other week, but I had many delays due to low counts that made the time longer.

During treatment, I was able to keep up with my schooling. The first year, I home schooled using some books that the school let me borrow. I did not feel that it was the right thing for me, so the first semester of this year I have been working from home, but getting assignments from my teachers at school. Second semester, I will return to school. I have decided to do the International Baccalaureate Program, and instead of struggling in tenth grade, I decided to go into ninth grade this year. From the work that I have done with the program so far, I find it fun and interesting and expect to stay through the full program.

Although the chemotherapy made it harder to practice my cello at times, I was still able to play the cello sometimes during treatment. In May of 1998, my brother Charlie and I had the honor of playing together at a friend's wedding. That was a lot of fun for me, and it was a milestone as it was the first time I have ever played for anything but a recital. I am practicing again now, and getting my strength back.

My off-treatment evaluation day was on December 2. That was a day of many tests to be sure that the cancer was completely gone. My idea was that it was somewhat like a track and field day, where one goes to each station and does the activity. This *was just a medical field day. All the tests went very well, and were 100% clear.*

*The last and most recent happening was my day surgery to take the mediport out. I had that on December 9. It was a short surgery, and I was only at the hospital for about four hours. The surgery went well, and the soreness is almost gone.*

*These days I am feeling great, and my strength has improved greatly. My hair is starting to grow back, and I am going back to my normal activities. I feel that I have learned a lot this past year, and feel that it made me stronger. I want to thank you again for keeping in touch to see how I was doing, and for your many kind thoughts and prayers.*

*Love, Danielle*

# MAKE A WISH!

When I was in the hospital during the first treatment, a volunteer from the Make-A-Wish Foundation visited, and told us they would like to grant a wish for me. My parents were initially panicked, as they thought wishes were only offered to terminally ill children, but they were quickly reassured that any child with a life-threatening illness was eligible. When asked what my wish was, I did not have to think for long. Since the fifth grade, I had wanted to see New York City, and kept a scrapbook of all things Broadway. Both my Uncle Bob and brother Charlie were musicians in Broadway shows, and I dreamt of playing the cello in one of those shows someday. I had watched every episode of "Rhoda" on TV Land, and when I lost my hair to chemotherapy, the Rhoda Morgenstern headscarf became a convenient fashion accessory. It was complemented by large hoop earrings, bell bottoms, and the best New York accent I could muster. So, the planning for a New York adventure began, and the result was the trip of a lifetime – filled with memorable moments to be cherished forever. Each day was packed with exciting new experiences, and each night I wrote about all of them.

## Day 1 – March 6, 1999

As promised, here is a short summary of what we did today. This morning, at 5:45am, a stretch limousine came into our driveway to pick us up. I was very surprised that it was a real limo, as I thought that when they said a limo would pick us up, it would be a Cadillac, not a stretch limo! This was all very exciting, as I had never previously been in a limo. It was very luxurious, and it was so nice to have space to stretch our legs out. The ride to the airport was very smooth. It was fun to be able to look across at my mom as I was talking to her. I enjoyed a nice glass of mineral water on the way down to Denver, as there were glasses and different beverages to drink with ice in the car. After arriving at the airport, we had a brief snack and drink at a cafe, and then went to our concourse. The flight was great too. It went very quickly, and we even arrived a bit early at LaGuardia Airport. When we arrived at LaGuardia, there was an even bigger limo waiting for us! This time it was a white one (the other was black), and it was about the size of two regular cars. We rode to the hotel in this one, and it was very difficult to see anything as the weather has not been beautiful. This limo had many champagne glasses and napkins. The hotel is wonderful. We are staying at a DoubleTree, and the room is very nice. There is a king bed, and a queen size pull-out bed in the main room. There is a big bathroom and a nice desk, that I am typing at right now. We did a lot of walking just for this first day. As I said earlier, the weather has not been great. It is very drizzly and rainy. We have gotten to use our umbrellas a lot. We first walked to the theater where we will see Titanic (the Broadway show) tomorrow.

We are going to be having brunch at a restaurant called "Ellen's Stardust Diner" and picked up our tickets today so there would be no need to rush tomorrow. We then came back to the hotel and my uncle called us. We met him for dinner at a nice Italian restaurant and everyone ate a lot. It was very good food, and irresistible. The final event of the evening was a trip to the top of the Empire State Building at night. It is a beautiful sight and was a lot of fun. I tried taking pictures, so I hope that they turn out! After spending about an hour there, we started the walk home. It seemed very long, as we had already done a great deal of walking. We stopped at a Starbucks along the way, and that revived us to make it back to the hotel. So that is where we are now, and I think I should be getting to bed now! It has been a big day. Till next time.

## Day 2 – March 7, 1999

Today was a very exciting and eventful day. We were a bit tired this morning from our trip and all that walking yesterday! So this morning was spent relaxing in the hotel room. It was beautiful weather outside today, but it was very chilly. There was a strong breeze that was ice cold – it looked like nice weather though! The Make-A-Wish Foundation made reservations for brunch today, and that was very fun and yummy. They were at a place called Ellen's Stardust Diner, and it appears to be a very popular place. There are big screens that show parts of movies and Broadway shows, and there is karaoke. The waiters and waitresses sing to the diners as they are eating. It is a lot of fun, and the people appear to be aspiring Broadway stars.

Their voices were very good. There was also a small train that went all the way around the inside of the restaurant. It was in between the top and bottom floors. Many posters were hung about the walls of women who had won the Miss Subway award, and also stars like Elvis. It was a very crazy place, and that made it very memorable. After lunch, we stopped briefly at the hotel to get some apparel better suited to the weather. It was a shock to step outside, as it was so cold! We then headed to the theater to see "Titanic." It was a wonderful show, and very engrossing. The music was nicely arranged and written, and the acting was very good. The theater where the show was is very historical. It was finished in 1909, and the first show to be there after the Depression was "The Sound of Music" with Mary Martin. During the Depression, it was used as a movie theater. At intermission, my brother's friend from the show came to us and told us that he had arranged to give us a backstage tour after the show, and that we could meet some of the performers. I was very excited about that! He left me with a darling teddy bear that he said some of the cast members wanted me to have. After the show, we ran to the stage door rather quickly and he escorted us right to the stage. All the performers had just finished taking their bows, and the curtain was down. They saw me, and the whole cast greeted me! It was very exciting, and I was sort of nervous. They all motioned for me to come stand with them, and someone took a group picture with the cast for me. It was great, and everyone was so nice. Afterwards, some people talked to me, and people said that they were very glad to meet me and that I could come to the show. I was very glad to be there! Another very exciting thing that happened was that the cast presented me with a "Titanic" poster that they had all signed. It is very neat, and I was very excited to receive it! Also, another friend of my brother's presented me with a score to the show. He said that I could look at it as I was listening, and also learn the cello part. I think that will be a lot of fun! So, the show was a very exciting experience. Unfortunately, the show has not earned the money needed to keep it going, and is closing in three weeks. However there is a tour that is traveling around the United States, and it is actually currently in Denver. The tour is not exactly the same as Broadway, as far as sets and such, but it has the same caliber of acting. Tonight we are just planning to go to dinner with my uncle, and relax. We are going to bed early, as we are expected at the Rosie O'Donnell show at 8:30 AM! It will be another fun and exciting day.

## Day 3 – March 8, 1999

Today was another very exciting and busy day. It started off by waking up early this morning in order to make it to the Rosie O'Donnell show. Unfortunately, the alarm clock time was an hour early, so we actually started getting ready at 5:30 AM instead of 6:30 AM. We realized this at about 6:00, so there was only a little extra time to sleep at that point. We had arranged a wakeup call for 6:30 AM, and had been wondering why it hadn't come, and sure enough, it came at the real 6:30. At 8:30 AM, the limousine was out front of the hotel waiting to pick us up. We rode the limo to NBC studio, and then waited. We did not find the Make-A-Wish representative, but finally were able to meet up with him while waiting for admittance to the studio. He was very nice. He has just recently finished treatment for non-Hodgkin's lymphoma too, and is getting tests done. Everything looks fine, and it is always great to meet someone else who has been through the same experience and come out victorious. When we were admitted into the studio, there were Ring Dings (HoHos) and milk on the chairs for the guests. Now it did not occur to us at the time, but later my dad came to the conclusion that these were meant to be eaten and make the audience hyper. We certainly needed some hyper attitudes, and a lot of energy for that show! It is very enthusiastic and active. There was also a free magazine – Sports Illustrated for Women. When everyone was settled, a man came out and started leading the audience in how to cheer and clap, and act crazy. It was a lot of fun, and pretty funny. He was a comedian named Joey Cole. His energy was amazing! He kept going throughout the whole show. The show was opened by a ten year old girl from Connecticut greeting the audience. She was very cute, and did some Irish step dancing for everyone. As the show got underway, it was wonderful! Rosie is so full of energy and jokes, and is a very entertaining person. The show featured Chaka Khan, Luke Perry (90210), and Kay Ballard. They were all very interesting people, and it was a fun show. At the end of the show, there is a box full of prizes that hovers around over the front part of the audience. Rosie and her friends try to hit the lever on the box, so that it will open and shower prizes on people, by shooting koosh balls from slingshots to hit it. It was looking like there would not be a hit, and then the box opened up right next to our row! We were able to collect some goodies. After the show, a line was formed to see Rosie, and get autographs and pictures. The people told me that I would be last, so that I could spend some time with Rosie. When my turn came, I was very excited. She was very easy to talk to, and just asked me general questions like my age, name, and what kind of cancer I had. When I said non Hodgkin's lymphoma, she said, "Well, guess what? Anyone who has had cancer gets a free jacket. If anyone asks you what was good about getting cancer, tell them that you got a free Rosie jacket." It was so nice of her! It is a nice denim jacket that has the logo written on it, and she signed it. She also signed a picture for me, and we got a picture of me with her. It was a very exciting experience, and I know that I will always remember it. After the Rosie show, we went to a couple places on our own – the French travel bureau and HMV records. HMV is a huge music store here. We found a nice deli to eat a little lunch at, and then decided to go to the village. When we arrived there, the first place that we went was Jerry Olinger's, which is a fabulous store full of celebrity pictures and memorabilia. I was very lucky there, and found some wonderful pictures of Valerie Harper (Rhoda) and The Carpenters. After that we went to meet my uncle, and later went to dinner at a nice, old restaurant in the village. It was called the Waverly Inn, and is very rustic looking inside. The food is very gourmet and yummy. We lingered there for quite a while, and then came back to the hotel. Well, it is about bedtime now. Tomorrow, it is not necessary to get up early, so we are going to take advantage of that! Tomorrow's big plan is seeing "The Scarlet Pimpernel".

## Day 4 – March 9, 1999

Today has been another busy day, as usual. We woke up late, and it was nice to get that extra sleep. However, that made breakfast a bit rushed. Today a tour of the Lincoln Center had been arranged, so that was the first thing we did (10:30 AM). That lasted until a little before noon, and was very interesting. The different theaters had interesting little facts and aspects. In the Symphony Hall, The New York Philharmonic was actually rehearsing, so we were able to hear a little bit of that. They sounded absolutely perfect. The performance hall is built in such a way that microphones are not needed, and the sound simply resonates. I thought that was very interesting to know. It is the same way in the ballet theater. In the Opera House theater, a rehearsal was also taking place. This one was for the "Queen of Spades." We observed from a high place separated by glass from the actual room. That was interesting too, and the lady told us something amazing. There are over four thousand seats in the house, and each one has a little computer that translates the words for the audience during a performance! So, the tour was fun. The lady leading it was very enthusiastic, and laughed a lot. She got along well with everyone, and told us that we were a nice bunch of people. She said that some of the groups she has get a bit irritated that they are not allowed to see some of the places in the complex. We saw many places though, and it was very interesting to learn some of the history and the way things work in the complex. After we were done with the tour, we walked around and found a nice little French restaurant for lunch. We spent a while there, and then caught a taxi to the Metropolitan Museum of Art. That place is magnificent. We went planning to see some Egyptian art and Monet, and were greatly rewarded with what we wanted! There were almost two full rooms of Monet, and many rooms of Egyptian art. I am doing a report for history class about Thutmose III, an apparently unknown pharaoh. Well, at the museum there was some information about him and Nefertiti, his stepmother, and also many statues and reliefs of each. It was very interesting to walk through the Egyptian exhibit, and as always, Monet's work was breathtaking. We stayed at the museum until it was time to leave for the hotel and get ready for the show. It was a very nice time. We had dinner downstairs, and that was very good. After, we all went to the theater for the show. "The Scarlet Pimpernel" was a very entertaining and funny show. It was very light and happy. My uncle came and gave us a backstage tour afterwards. We took a picture of me by the guillotine that is used in the show. I have not been feeling so well tonight. There is a pain in my stomach and I have been having bad headaches. Hopefully those will go away soon. I must be eating too much good food! Tomorrow's plans are exciting. We are going to go on a limo ride around the city from 11:00 AM to 3:00 PM. We're going to pick up a friend of ours, and she will come with us. That will be fun. Well, I should hit the sack now. We switch hotels now, so I will be writing from a different place. We will stay there until our Saturday afternoon flight.

## Day 5 – March 10, 1999

Today was the day of our exciting limousine ride. A family friend came to meet us just as we were finishing breakfast this morning. She came along to share the ride. We had the limousine from 11:00 AM to 3:00 PM. It was a lot of fun. The first place that we went was the obelisk of Thutmose III in Central Park, Cleopatra's Needle. It was amazing, and I was glad to be able to see it. It is very tall and outstanding. It was transported here from Alexandria, and has suffered some damage. It says in the New York Access book that the hieroglyphics on the obelisk had lasted for 3,500 years, and when it was transported to New York, the hieroglyphics disintegrated due to the pollution. We all thought this was an amazing and awful fact. After that we went to Battery Park. There, we saw a Korean War memorial. It was very interesting. There was also a huge fort there that was never actually used, but was transferred there for viewing. It is called Clinton Castle. There was also a great view of the Statue of Liberty and the other islands out in the harbor. When we had finished at Battery Park, we drove across the Brooklyn Bridge into Brooklyn. That was great to drive over that bridge. On the other side, we got out and walked for awhile. It seemed nice, and it was interesting for me as I read the book "A Tree Grows in Brooklyn." By the time we had come back from that side, it was time to start towards the new hotel (the one that my parents arranged to extend our stay beyond the wish trip). Now my parents had been telling me that we would be staying at the "Econodump" as it would be hard to afford anything else. Last night was the last night of the actual Make-A-Wish trip, and that is why we have switched hotels. Well, the limo driver pulled up in front of the Plaza Hotel, and I figured that we were just temporarily stopping there. Well, we were there to stay! As a surprise, my parents made reservations at The Plaza for the rest of the time. It is an absolutely wonderful hotel, although very posh. It is very fun to be here though! After arriving at the hotel, we had a little snack to hold us until dinner. Then, we talked with my uncle and arranged that we would meet him and go to dinner. We went to a nice Italian restaurant called Ralph's. After that, we went to the theater for the show. Tonight, we saw my uncle's show, "Captain's Courageous." It was a great show, and very family-oriented. A funny thing happened during the show, and my uncle had told us to listen to the part where people call out the names of ships. Well, sure enough, the ships that they called out to the audience were the Sara Jane, Danielle DuChateau, Kara K, and Paul Christian. That was fun. After the show we were able to meet all the actors, and they all seemed very nice. Well, I need to hit the sack now. It is 12:30am! So, I will sink into the comfortable bed now, which someone has turned back in preparation. (That happened while we were gone) I will write again tomorrow!

## Day 6 – March 11, 1999

Today was a rather calm day, and we did not attempt so much as in previous days. We just did what came to mind, and still had a lot of fun. Make-A-Wish is not scheduling our activities for the rest of the time, as we have extended our trip these couple of days. The first thing that we did this morning was go to a bowmaker's office that is on Broadway just near Columbus Circle. My cello teacher wanted us to go there as my cello bow needs re-hairing. He was very nice, and is going to fix my bow for me. It needs re-hairing, as well as some weight added to it. The bow is very light, and that makes it harder to play as well as not achieving the best sound possible. The bowmaker will ship it back to us a week from now. After going there, we were looking for a breakfast place. Fortunately, there was a Starbucks nearby, and we were able to go there. It has been so bitterly cold that we are glad to go inside often. After having a nice breakfast, we walked over to Central Park. I saw a pretzel stand, and decided that we had to take advantage of that at least once during our visit. I went up to buy one, and used my best New York accent on the guy. It was fun. My mom's friend had told us that there was a nice zoo inside the park. It is not very big, but that was one of the nice things about it. It is very easy to walk through the whole zoo in about an hour. We were there during the feeding time for the sea lions. That was a lot of fun to watch. We met my mom's friends for dinner. They took us to a very nice Italian restaurant. It was a small place, and appeared to be family owned. It was the kind of place where all the family recipes are cooked. So, we had a nice dinner there. After we came outside of the restaurant, the wind had really picked up. It was freezing cold and very strong! As we were looking for a cab, the wind literally blew me off my feet. I fell right on my hip, and my parents had to help me up. Fortunately, I did not hurt anything. I just have a bruise and some soreness. Well, we found a cab right after that and returned to the hotel. That is the point that I am at now. It was a good day. Tomorrow is the last day here, so I am sure that it will be fun. We are going to have tea in the Palm Room at the hotel, so that should be posh and fun. Until then!

## Day 7 – March 12, 1999

It has been a late night (it is 1am), so this will be a short one. Tonight's newsletter ends the vacation, as our flight home leaves tomorrow afternoon. I am sorry to leave, but it will be nice to get home. I also have so many memories to take home with me. I am so glad that I chose this vacation for my wish, and it was very well fulfilled! Today, we had breakfast at a nice, little, healthy place. After that we went to see Radio City Music Hall, but were disappointed to find that it is not possible. It is under remodeling now, and is not open to anyone. I was sorry to find that out, but I will make it one of these days! After that, we went to the theater where "Titanic" was playing to drop off some thank-you notes. I wanted to write one to the company for everything that they did, and my mom also wrote one. We had a nice lunch at a restaurant called Sardi's, which is right by Broadway and is a popular place for famous people. Until late afternoon, we walked around a lot looking for some carry-on bag that was a reasonable price. We have much more to bring home than we took, and need a little extra storage space for the trip home. It is amazing what the stores try to charge for everything! I have a feeling they charge a higher price than what the product is really worth, but we found a store where the guy worked the price down to $25, which is still a bit much, but we were tired and decided to take it. We rested in the hotel room until we were ready for dinner. It felt good to sit down after all that walking! We went to my uncle's show again tonight, and I sat in the pit this time. That was a lot of fun. I was able to sit next to the cellist, who is very good. He has studied with Leonard Rose. A lot of funny things happened in the pit because the musicians goof around during the show. Most of all, my uncle. (The conductor, of all people!) After the show there was a celebration for my uncle as today is his birthday. The company got him a cake, and gave him some presents. After that was all over, we went out for late night drinks with my uncle and one of the writers of the show. My uncle has a friend who let us into his restaurant even though it was closed. We stayed there a little over an hour, and I was not surviving so well. So, we left awhile after. So, that is the end to our great trip! I will write again when I return home.

★★★

*I'm not sure if anything will ever be normal again – or if it even should be. I can't just forget everything that happened, or everyone I knew. I think I had a sense of security when we were actively fighting cancer during treatment, but now I have to check my neck, armpits and groin for swollen lymph nodes each day when I wake up, and before bed. It felt like the whole world was there to support me during treatment, but now I feel completely alone. I don't know what's wrong with me because sometimes I feel like everything will be alright, but sometimes I'm not sure it will be. I look forward to returning to school, and having more trivial concerns – like cramming for exams, or doing my hair that is growing back. The teachers at orientation night seemed really nice; but I saw MT from orchestra, and she didn't recognize me at first — and when she did, she walked away so I couldn't talk to her. Everything changed when I was diagnosed, and everything changed during treatment — and I'm not sure how I will adjust and fit in again. Sometimes I'm not sure how to move on, like everyone else, and pretend that everything is fine again. I will try to stay positive though.*

## Friday, January 1, 1999

It is the first day of 1999, and I am still in the last year. Oh well, it will take awhile to get used to this new year, and all the new opportunities it holds. Since treatment is over now, I will need to adjust myself back to my "regular" lifestyle. It has not been difficult thus far. I will be returning to school on January 19th, and that will be the biggest thing to adjust to, I believe.

## Saturday, January 16, 1999

Haven't written in a long time. Today I worked on French. I am a bit behind. I am a bit worried about having my 5-minute speech. I have to talk about myself for five minutes! Last week I went to school for two days for the world game, and activities the next day. It was a lot of fun and the students at Poudre are nice. I already have lots of friends. On Wednesday I had a doctor's checkup, and everything looks good. My mother and I went to get my schedule on Thursday. It looks good, and I have two free periods! I am so looking forward to starting school.

## Misfit

Can you see my faultiness,
My common lack of hope?
The strangely off-track feeling,
And the inability to cope?
I'm not the normal person
You may think I am.
Nothing special, nothing perfect.
No rare and special gem.
My thoughts are much too deep,
Too perverted and too strange.
How I long to be like you,
But now I cannot change.
I don't know what is right,
And I don't know what is wrong.
I don't know what is popular,
Or the latest new hit song.
A misfit in the crowd,
A stranger to humanity.
Have you never noticed me -
Verging on insanity?


## Fragile

A miniscule part of humanity,
Afraid of all the rest;
Yet also afraid of itself.
One crushing blow,
And everything is done.
As a shooting star,

*This brightness*
*Loses light and splendor —*
*As it is broken down.*
*A wish to save it,*
*And keep it safe from the world.*
*Forever.*

## The Monster Within Me

*The monster within me is hidden from the world —*
*A dark side that nobody can see.*
*A part that is secret, lonely, and painful —*
*A soul that longs to be free.*
*A voice that tells me I'm worthless,*
*And cannot do anything right;*
*That I deserve to hurt and starve,*
*And never see the light.*
*The monster within me pushes me down,*
*And it seems I can never rise.*
*It tells me I will never be good enough,*
*And brings tears that sting my eyes.*
*The monster tells me I will never be well,*
*Or healthy and free again.*
*It tells me to work, and never relax,*
*And that having fun is a sin.*
*The monster within me tells me that*
*I can do nothing less than perfection.*
*It leads me to hate all that I do,*
*And says I'm beyond correction.*
*I'm not pretty, successful, or deserving.*
*I'm not as good as another.*

*Since nothing can ever be good enough,*
*Why should I even bother?*
*How did I survive instead of someone else*
*Who was also fighting cancer?*
*Why did I deserve to live?*
*I still cannot find the answer.*
*The monster within makes me hate myself,*
*And everything to do with me.*
*It obliterates the positives,*
*And all the good I could be.*

## Tuesday, September 21, 1999

Nobody understands. Nobody understands what it is like to live with cancer in my past. They cannot and they will not. Everyone has forgotten and everything is forgotten. Except by me. I remember everything. But I cannot express any feelings without criticism or questioning. What is wrong?! My cancer is still a vivid memory – it is thought of every night. I am the only one who thinks about that memory. You can't keep people here on earth. Anything could happen. Every day I think about the patients I knew who didn't make it – and how I wish it were me instead of them. I wish I could bring them back because I feel like they would appreciate life so much more. I feel like I am doubly ungrateful and undeserving since I survived cancer, and I can't deal with living. My friend tells me to just get over it and that I am alright. My parents and brothers tell me that I am alright. I don't feel alright and I don't know what would make things better because I can never share this pain with anyone else and it is unacceptable to feel this way. What did

I put my parents through? I hate to think of all the pain they may not have been able to express. I am afraid they were too scared to ever talk about their feelings about my illness, in the worry that they would upset me. Is it comparable to all this pain that I feel? I would never want anyone else to suffer this.

## Random Thoughts

*Sometimes I want to laugh,*
*And sometimes I want to cry.*
*Sometimes I feel very hopeful,*
*And sometimes I want to die.*
*My feelings often seem like a chaos,*
*That can never be resolved and made neat.*
*Sometimes I feel like it's over,*
*And every day is just a repeat.*
*Sometimes I feel out of control,*
*As if my mind has gone into a craze.*
*Other times my heart feels empty,*
*And my mind seems to enter a daze.*
*Sometimes I feel so lonely,*
*When nobody can understand.*
*I know that they may try,*
*Yet nobody ever can.*
*Sometimes I have dark thoughts,*
*That scare me and I cannot share;*
*I wish I could express those feelings,*
*Because maybe someone would care.*
*Sometimes I want to crawl in a hole,*
*And pull it in after me.*
*I feel like I'm lost in the dark,*
*Looking for a future I can't see.*

## October 11, 1999

It seems so insensitive to type a journal entry but there are so many things going on in my head right now that to write by hand would take far too long. I should not even be wasting the time writing this shit at all because I have an exam tomorrow and I have not studied one bit for it. I am in denial or maybe I just gave up on myself. I do not really care. There is another exam on Thursday and I probably will not study for that one either. It feels like something has snapped and I cannot even connect with anyone today. I want to connect with someone because it feels like a safety concern at this point, but I have staved off actually doing it. I am never quite sure why I do this. My parents have given me everything and I do not deserve any of it. I should be getting off my ass and studying instead of writing this shit. I haven't felt quite right all day from the moment I woke up I was just off kilter and then the events of the day fucked things up even more. Talking to my friend was just a diversion. I don't know what I want. I don't know who I'm interested in. I don't know how to communicate like a normal human being. All I can think about right now is how do I get out of this how do I get out of this. Out of the exams? Out of having to interact with people? Out of life? I don't expect everything to be good. It would be a nice surprise if you're not expecting it but like my new approach to everything in life, if you don't expect anything or expect the worst then the blow when it comes is not as severe. It doesn't always work in practice, but in theory it sounds practical. So I've come to the end of my patience with writing and god knows what shit I've written but I guess

I feel like a miniscule amount of pressure was relieved. I found a Sylvia Plath quote today that kind of sums up how I feel: "Perhaps when we find ourselves wanting everything, it is because we are so dangerously near to wanting nothing."

## Monday, February 21, 2000

I feel like I cannot go on. Is life really worth living? There is so much sorrow, and everything seems so hopeless. My aunt passed away from her battle with cancer yesterday – we received the call this morning. Nothing is fair. Life is a deceiving thing. How are we to survive if our own bodies deceive us?!?! Where is the "land of milk and honey"? It certainly does not seem like it is anywhere on this earth. Why did I survive cancer? All these other wonderful people did not deserve to die, and had great lives ahead of them. Where is the judgment, why is this such a struggle? I am scared – so damn scared of the doctor finding something at the checkup seven days from now. I am going to be a total wreck this week. I cannot help it. I live with nightmares of death and daydreams of chemotherapy. I cannot run from real life in sleep and I cannot run from the horrible nightmares in daylight. Life will never return to "normal". Normal does not exist. It will never be the same again. People say that one can choose full life or worry of relapse. That is no choice! It is always at the forefront of the mind and there sure as hell is no choice in thinking about it!

_Pain_

_A sickness in my stomach,_
_A pain in my chest;_
_An ache in my heart,_
_And little peaceful rest._
_Constant worry in my mind,_
_And hatefulness in my head._
_A hope to stay alive,_
_Yet wishing to be dead._
_No hope to live much longer,_
_Yet wishing for many more years._
_The pain has settled in –_
_Bringing with it unrelentless tears and fears._
_Stop this hurting please –_
_I think I cannot go on._
_Will my hopeless soul_
_Ever see a bright new dawn?_

## March 1, 2000

I do not have any power and I need to get a handle on things. I feel so incompetent right now, useless, exhausted, as if I should not even be breathing air on this earth. If there is any survival of the fittest law I should be eliminated. I can't control my anger any more and I can't let people know about it either. I just feel sick. I feel physically sick but I feel emotionally sick too, kind of like when your character's health points run out in a game and they die...

*Please stop the world,*
*I want to get off —*
*I cannot take any more.*
*Everything is down,*
*The sky is falling,*
*And living life is a chore.*
*It is spinning too quickly, and I cannot see,*
*Where the hell I'm going.*
*I wish I saw what others see,*
*But maybe it is better not knowing.*
*We have passed the limit enough for a ticket,*
*And we are moving too fast.*
*Some are cruelly flung away,*
*As the rest attempt to last.*
*The glorious world is a monster,*
*Devouring its next of kin.*
*Do not attempt to beat the game —*
*Because there is no way to win.*

## April 29, 2000

Writing with my new, totally awesome gel pen here. I am not even quite sure what to say, but I feel compelled to write something. Trying to move on is a bitch. No matter how much fun or how miserable an experience with friends is, you still have to come home and face yourself. You have to feel the sudden emptiness that would be there whether or not you were with people. I felt like cutting tonight. If my body looked how I feel inside, it would be black and disintegrated, bloodied from its experiences and suffering from irreparable damage. Emotional pain doesn't speak, it just hurts.

## Saturday, May 13, 2000

Well, May 28 is quickly approaching again and it has been harder than ever for me to stay collected and not worry about the anniversary of discovery and diagnosis. Today was a bad sign. I feel so confused and worried right now. We went to the hospital today because I have swollen lymph nodes again. We had a lot of blood tests done, chest x-rays, and some examinations. Suggestion? Just come back Monday for the regular scheduled checkup and have a CT scan done as well. I have been absolutely pooped the rest of today.

## Tuesday, May 16, 2000

I feel like shit today, and totally self-abusive. My checkup yesterday was "fine," and actually the prognosis is very good. The doctor saw nothing on the CT scan, and my blood counts actually look good. A lot of things point to the conclusion that the only thing that may be wrong is that I have a viral infection. I know this is something more serious, but nobody cares. I have been thinking I am sick again for months now, but I do not care anymore. I do not deserve to be well. I wish people would stop saying everything is good with my health because I know something is wrong. I just want to die because I will never be normal. All I will ever be is sick, and I know what I am writing here is probably just another example of being sick. What is wrong with me? Everyone says that I am negative, but I think that it is a lot more than that. Nobody cares if everything seems okay when it's not. If I die maybe someone will believe me, but then it will be too late, won't it? Who cares… I know these are some pretty upset words – but I could not keep them in any longer. I have to have that biopsy on Friday – because I cannot just "get over" this…

## The Unknown Struggle

*How can loneliness and depression sink in,*
*When the prognosis for life is so high?*
*Why must the days seem so long and a struggle,*
*As precious life is now racing by?*
*The unseen fear, and the unseen trouble,*
*Now have their time at hand;*
*They beg to torture,*
*And kill the soul,*
*With the attention they command.*
*There can be no understanding, or any rest,*
*From this fear that has taken hold;*
*But the feelings are not the facts, and so,*
*Can never be truthfully told.*
*So this is a poem that attempts to describe*
*A struggle of unbelievable dread.*
*At times life can seem so pointless, and hopeless,*
*And living no better than dead.*

## Friday, May 19, 2000

I had the lymph node biopsy today, and when Dr. S. came to tell us afterwards that it looked suspicious, it confirmed what I already know in my heart – the cancer has come back. However, everyone still has hope that it is merely a virus. Dr. S. said that she will know and call with the final diagnosis on May 26. It will be one of the longest week of my life.

\*\*\*

*Every moment in the waiting room of the oncology clinic feels like an eternity. The receptionist still knows us well, but I'm not sure if she knows why we are here, on this particular day. It may be a long-term follow-up appointment because I have been in remission for a year and a half. That is considered a relatively safe amount of time in remission, if not yet out of the woods. But I am not here for a follow-up. Dr. S. comes out personally to take us back. We go to the last room on the right, in the hallway of exam rooms, just outside the infusion room. It is the small room with a few chairs, a small table, and a box or two of tissues. It is the room where you go for difficult conversations. The results of the lymph node biopsy have already been disclosed over the phone…at least to my parents, who had the courage to listen. Even before the surgery, I knew what the results of the biopsy would be, and I did not want to hear them spoken aloud. I'm not sure how much I'm hearing of the conversation, but I hear Dr. S. saying not to worry because there are still options left in the bag of tricks. I think to myself that the cancer coming back after such a long time must be a cruel trick, but there is no surprise reveal, since I felt it take hold of my body again. I think to myself that you can't trick cancer because it is the trickiest thing there is – tricky to diagnose, tricky to treat, and tricky to survive – with any normal quality of life after treatment. I put up my strong façade, like this is all just peanuts, and I'm an old pro. I am an old pro, but even when you bolster yourself with past experience, and pretend like something doesn't bother you, it still does.*

## Sunday, May 28, 2000

My world is turned upside down once again… Words seem inadequate to describe this, as one of my friends says. A lot of shit has gone down in the past couple of weeks. I had surgery to put in a broviac, do a spinal tap, and check my bone marrow. I felt pretty bad after the surgery, but feel better today. I think I am sinking – lower and lower. I feel so hopeless and helpless. Why this again?? I can't believe it. If someone wants me dead so badly, or near it, why don't they just kill me. I feel so many times that I am not worth this trouble or money. I feel suicidal to be truthful. I can't stand feeling like such a burden!! I hate myself, and I cannot stop. I feel like just giving up. This is not worth it. It's hell. I just wanna die. Funny thing to say on a birthday… I have been amazed at the support that I have found from my peers. Numerous people have dropped by with cards and gifts, and it is just amazing. I never thought so many people cared about me. Well, I am getting tired now. I will try and write more positively later.

## *Relapse*

*I feel you in every thought —*
*Threatening to replay the past.*
*I feel the pain and helplessness,*
*Of an existence that cannot last.*
*Swelling up with strength,*
*I shudder under your force.*
*Come back to me, come back again —*
*Go on and run your course.*

## Thursday, June 15, 2000

Here I am, finally writing something. It's no wonder. My emotions have gone completely haywire today. I don't feel like I can handle anything, and everything is getting my goat! I feel like killing myself again. People can laugh all they want. I know they do — I hear them right now! They can laugh themselves to death. Why do I feel so bad now? I am being so mean! Well, I have been having awful nightmares again. They are all different, and yet the same. I die in every one of them. In one, I was shot down at school and lying in a pool of blood. Nobody bothered to help me, and I died in solitude. In the next dream I was at school and these military people invaded. They called names over the intercom, and those students were gunned down by machine guns against a wall. I woke as the bullet was entering. I recognized the other patients in one that happened at some camp place but all I remember is we were dying from AIDS. In the last one, I was in a big house. The rooms were huge, and there had been other girls there, but they were gone. The rooms had names, girls names, and

I think that they were named after the girls who lived in them. But I don't know what happened to the other girls. I was all alone, and I didn't know what to do, when a girl who survived whatever happened came to tell me I needed to leave or I would be put to death. And then I woke up. Well, that is probably enough of my perverseness for one night. What is wrong with me and how can I fix this?!?

## The End

*Sink down further and further —*
*The fall is not long,*
*And yet it lasts for an eternity.*
*Blackness.*
*Darkness envelops the vision,*
*And thoughts of death shake the mind.*
*The heart aches, and the tears*
*Are a fountain of sorrow.*
*No love is there, and no hope.*
*What is there to live for,*
*And where is life itself?*
*Pretending there is a rose-colored world,*
*That does not even exist.*
*The image is nice —*
*When you can keep it.*
*Eventually when you're not looking,*
*The good feeling flies away, free —*
*Free — as you long to be.*
*The toxic pity saturates the soul,*
*And pulls it, and everything else down.*
*Down to the bottom of life.*
*The end.*

## Saturday, June 17, 2000

After some thought, I have decided that it is the time to write about some of what has happened, from the beginning until right now. It all began on Saturday, May 13, which was the day after A's birthday party. I woke up and did my routine checkup of my neck. I was shocked to find that there was a swollen lymph node, just above my collarbone. It was not big, but I began to sob because I had a bad feeling about it. We called the hospital, as I had a routine checkup on Monday, May 15th anyway. They suggested we come down right away for some tests. They said that they were not sure, so Saturday did not offer any closure or relief from what I knew was bad. I had a "suspicious" lymph node biopsy on Friday, May 19th and Friday, May 26th was the day of the call with the final diagnosis. I felt as if I was at a funeral all day long during school and broke down in front of Ms. K. That is how low my heart had sunk, and how deep my depression had become. When I came home, I jumped every time the telephone rang, and tears would come to my eyes. I was hysterical. Finally, I settled down distractedly and began to work on math homework. The phone rang, and from the way my mother answered and the way my father went to get on the other phone, I knew it was Dr. S. I could not move, and I could not bring myself to get on and listen. I began to sob because I knew what was happening in my heart. When my parents got off the phone and began walking towards me, I knew definitely. They did not say the actual words, but we all kind of laughed through tears as my father said, "Well, you don't have to worry about that stupid algebra homework." I notified family and friends by email and telephone, and the time is but a memory of endless phone calls, and emotional chaos for me. It was really, really difficult to appreciate my birthday – a day seemingly so cursed that it has come to signify a bad omen every year. Although there was much fun and festivity, and a beaming Danielle on the outside, I felt a sinking feeling on the inside – a helplessness I cannot explain. I had the idea of the beginning of chemotherapy treatment the next day in my mind the whole day. The reality had been quite dormant in my mind while the celebration was going on, but by night a feeling of dread began to pervade my being. I could not believe that this was really happening again. It was like a nightmare I could not escape. Charlie and Annbritt had flown in to surprise me for the big day, and that indeed lightened my mood. On Monday, May 29th, chemotherapy treatment began. I smiled and assured everyone that everything was fine, but a lot of times one cannot be sure of their own words in their heart. I did reassure myself that all would be fine and that treatment would not be that bad. All those assurances seemed to fail when I got to the hospital. Merely sitting in the room on my bed caused me to gag and retch. I was not even hooked up to fluids yet – it was merely the association of hospital = chemotherapy and vice versa. Charlie and Annbritt called about dinner and the mere thought of food or drink at the hospital made me retch – and it was Noodles & Company – one of my favorites. They brought me some nice, plain, buttered noodles, but I was already too sick to eat what they had so thoughtfully brought. Everyone had to clear the room to go eat their food because it made me feel too sick. All I could do was puke and cry and think that as much as I had prepared myself for what going back into treatment would be like, it was not any easier. I had been on IV fluids for a couple of hours, and then it was chemotherapy time. The nurse came in with a bag of ARA-C and the room got silent. I felt like crying out, "You can't do this to me!" but my face stayed without emotion. After the nurse had left I began to retch and cry. I could not help it. The thought of that poison going into my body again made me feel sick. Christian came too and my family did a grand job of distracting me with an animated game of charades. It was a fun time, and kept my mind off the present situation for awhile. The next two days are an unpleasant blur of nausea, depression, and not feeling good in general. People came and went from the hospital room, but none of it meant anything to me in the state that I was in. I had a bone scan on Wednesday, which was very difficult. I was strapped down on a table, forbidden to move, while my stomach continued its attempts of turning inside out in revolt to the chemotherapy. When I returned from the bone scan, a resident came in to take out the stiches from my surgery. Overcome with all the feelings and events of the whole stay, I could no longer hold my emotions inside. I began to cry uncontrollably, and this is the state that Dr. S found me in. She studied me for a bit, and then commented that perhaps what I needed was a really good cry, and sometimes I think she was right! I was allowed to be discharged Wednesday night. Given the choice to stay or leave, as I was still quite sick, I did not have to think for a moment's time before deciding to leave. I would rather be sick in the comfort of home than the hospital.

Who wouldn't? I felt as if I was escaping torture when I left the hospital. After a time of thinking, I told everyone that I did not know that a person could feel so awful. I did not know such pain and discomfort could be felt before death. A friend said cancer is so paradoxical, and I agree. One must feel worse before they can feel better. My daily shots began on Friday. Those were not too bad, as I was used to them from the previous treatment. The day more unpleasantness broke loose was Tuesday. I had to begin antibiotics, and they made me feel as sick as chemotherapy. Around 10:30 AM, I found that I could not get enough air to fall asleep, and my chest was restricted with every breath. I panicked and we went to Dr. B. He did not see or hear anything serious, but suggested that we have a chest x-ray done just in case. When I got to the hospital, I was overcome by an awful wave of nausea, hotness, and a faint feeling. I thought I would pass out. I believe it can be attributed to the antibiotics. I stayed on the antibiotic Cipro until Saturday, and the antibiotic Biaxin (that had been switched for Augmentin) until Monday, when we returned to the oncology clinic. I had a checkup, and we went to the dreaded conference room, where Dr. S told us some more details of the treatments and procedures I would have. We returned to the clinic on Thursday for counts, and were shocked to find that my ANC was 18!! During my previous treatment, the lowest that my ANC had gone was 500, so this was a totally new experience. I had a platelet transfusion, and we were to return on Monday. The best part was that I was given permission to discontinue the antibiotics! When we returned on Monday, my ANC was nearly 10,000, and my platelets had recovered themselves. The doctor was amazed at how quickly and how well my immune system had recovered. I have been able to see friends and do things throughout this week. What a blessing it is just to be able to go outside, walk about, visit with friends, and have the energy to do things that one wants to do!

## Sunday, June 18, 2000

Well, I am here to dish out some emotions before the next treatment. I am beginning to have that sense of dread about treatment tomorrow. I am having a spinal tap and two days of chemotherapy in the clinic. Funny that we should have to go to the hospital the day after Mother's Day and the day after Father's Day too... I played my cello for the first time in a little over a month yesterday. It felt awkward and I had the usual feelings of failure and hysteria at the sorry state that my playing had come to. Today, I played with my accompanist. We were both thrilled to be playing again. Although I could not play that well, she was very understanding, and we had a lot of laughs. We went for coffee afterwards, and had a nice chat. My thoughts and fears about treatment escaped me, and I can no longer contain it all as well. Sometimes I feel so helpless and wonder what the point of going through this again is. Other times I have the most uplifting and happy feeling. I feel like a puppet, or as if I have a facade in front of me. I am all smiles even if I feel like crap because I do not want anyone to know. I want to be strong. I want to succeed. I want to be good, and not cause concern.

## Monday, June 26, 2000

The last treatment was pretty difficult, but I did not have the full unpleasant impact of it until some time after. The first day began with hydration and Zofran, and progressed to a spinal tap and lots of chemo. During the time of the spinal I was receiving six drugs at once (hydrocortisone, Decadron, Cytoxan, daunorubicin, methotrexate, and ARA-C). Needless to say, I felt very nauseous and uncomfortable by the end of the first day. The second day was better. I hardly felt nauseous, and the bone marrow transplant doctor, Dr. G., came in to talk to us. He was very nice, and put our minds a bit more at ease concerning the whole bone marrow transplant process. It still sounds scary, but at least now I have some idea of what I am getting myself into. I am having what is called an autologous stem cell transplant, which means that I am using my own and not a donor's. It will be a long process with lots of preparation and lots of aftermath, but if it will make me well, then it is all worth it! So, that is what happened at the second treatment.

## Monday, July 3, 2000

Thought I would write a bit today. Everything is going well. Received the good news that I do not have to go in for the surgery to put the stem cell harvest catheter in until Monday, rather than this Friday, so one more free weekend! I have been feeling well enough, although at times waves of fatigue hit me. I just began wearing the wig again a couple of days ago. It makes me feel like a real person with hair again. I have been controlling of my appetite so that I do not swell and have stretch marks again, even though I am well off steroids. Taking walks and playing the cello are good diversions for me. I feel stiff and tired. Time for bed.

## Friday, July 7, 2000

Not too much happened today. I feel tired all the time, and never seem to have the bursts of energy that used to come. I have trouble getting enough sleep, and the summer days only serve to worsen this with their annoying stickiness. Double GCSF shots began today, in preparation for my stem cell harvest. I could not have had the shot more than four hours ago, and I already feel it in my back and hips. I guess I can be thankful that the surgery for the pick line was not today. It would have ruined my weekend.

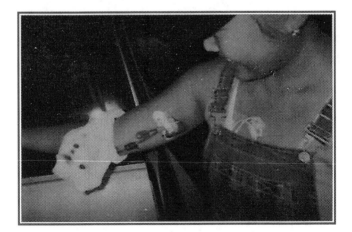

## Sunday, July 9, 2000

I feel okay today, but I do not feel like eating and I have a throbbing headache. My body still feels exhausted, and I cannot seem to do much of anything. I am a bit scared about tomorrow, which is the surgery to put the stem cell pick line in my arm. The actual collection of the stem cells should not be too bad. I cannot help but think about the chemotherapy treatment at the end of the week. It is like the first one I had, where I said that I could not have imagined anyone had the capacity to feel so bad. I get to spend the weekend in the hospital. At least I get to watch movies during the week!

## Friday, July 14, 2000

Of course the first thing that comes to mind is that this is Bastille Day for the French, which is where we are supposed to be this summer. Oh well – on to the many stories that I have to tell you about this week! It has been a long, long week, but it is over! Monday was surgery day to put in the apheresis catheter. We were gravely mistaken to call it a pick line – the doctor in interventional radiology made that very clear to us. We went to the oncology clinic, and were then sent downstairs to interventional radiology. The procedure was done in the same room as the broviac. Beforehand, I was asked whether I would rather be awake or asleep during the procedure. I said asleep, and it was agreed that I would receive Fentanyl and another drug that I had before called Nembutal. As my parents left and the procedure began, I was waiting for the anesthetic to take its effect. I felt dizzy when the nurse injected the Fentanyl, but then it wore off quickly. I felt the prick in my arm and my pulse quickened. I must have flinched, as the doctor said "Did that hurt?" I said yes, and was given more Fentanyl. The drugs never had their effect though, and I was awake during the entire procedure. When, at one point, the doctor began pushing hard into my upper arm, I began to cry and the remainder of the operation was a struggle. After the operation, I was wheeled into a room to wait for thirty minutes for the dizziness to subside. We went back up to the clinic to confirm everything for the next day, and then drove to Charlie's. I was awfully tired, but still felt like going to dinner. I felt like an idiot – a helpless one. I could not walk on my own and needed my father's help. In addition to this my broviac tube was protruding from my tank top while my pain from the operation caused me to hold my arm wayward. Tuesday morning, we went to the blood bank in the downstairs of the hospital, as that was where the harvest took place. When we arrived, there were three people waiting for us – a doctor and two nurses. My catheter site was looked at, and the nurses were shocked at the amount of blood around it. I was hooked up to the gargantuan machine. It was absolutely amazing! I had a double lumen catheter, so one side was hooked up for taking my blood, and the other for receiving the blood. The machine took my blood and separated it into stem cells, platelets, and red cells. It took my stem cells, and returned as much as possible of red cells and platelets. As the machine was so large, the only choice for activities seemed to be watching movies or television. So, we chose movies. There was an extensive list that made it comparable to going to the movie store and choosing one. We had a Robin Williams fest, and watched Awakenings and The Dead Poet's Society. They were good. The first day we had a 1.4 yield, which sounded unfortunately small compared to the eight that we needed. Wednesday, we returned at 8am again for another round. We watched The Shining and had a 1.9 yield. Thursday, we watched Caddyshack and Sense & Sensibility, and had a 1.6 yield. Friday – today – we watched the funniest commercials and played Trivial Pursuit. I do not know what my yield is, but I know we did not make it. We went up to the clinic today as we have been doing every day, but today was a day of some decisions – would I need a platelet transfusion, did I need more harvesting, and should we pull the catheter. We waited for a long time, and finally the doctors and the BMT nurse came in. Then I knew that the line was coming out. Sure enough, one doctor was there to pull it and the other confirmed the decision. Although we did not get as many stem cells as Dr. G. wanted, he said that he was discontinuing harvesting for now. We may need to do more following the next chemo treatment, but I sure hope not. The harvesting process was alright, but it certainly made me tired. And, I ate a lot and feel really bad about that. My arm is sore from pulling the catheter. I did not cry when it was pulled. I promised myself that I would not, and I kept it. It was about ten inches long!

## Saturday, July 15, 2000

So lonely, and yet, it is as if the whole world is rooting for you... Many cards and telephone calls and presents that are blindly answered and received. There is a depression within that cannot be placed – it is the pain that cannot be spoken of. This is a different planet, and contact with those of normal lives seems so difficult at times. Will the torture ever end? It is easy to face the monster in the day, but what about the night? Death rears its head, and as tears stream and fear creeps in, there is nobody. Death tries to have its way in either direction. Pick your poison or choose nothing, and death is there to try. Lonely, depressed, afraid of darkness...

## Sunday, July 16, 2000

Not too much excitement today. We went for a walk. I do not know what is wrong. I cannot feel interested in anything. It is the same as always – smiling on the outside, crying on the inside. My accompanist came to play with me today. It was fun, although I cannot play well anymore. I have been feeling a deep depression within – it feels as if there is a great void. I do not know how to fill it. Sometimes it seems like I try to fill it with food. I cannot control my eating any more. It seems to have gone haywire with everything else. We go for the next inpatient chemo treatment tomorrow. I am not looking forward to that.

## Saturday, July 29, 2000

I have felt the need to write for a long time, and yet there is so much to say that I worry that it will not all be recorded. My most deep and important thoughts enter my mind in the night, or during some other time when it is not possible to write. My hands are weak and struggle to form the words in my head properly onto paper. I am at an emotional low point now. I do not know what is wrong. I feel scared – I have a bad feeling within that I cannot explain. My worry and the bad feeling are making me lie awake in the nights, pondering. Sometimes I wonder what my fate is – if there is a happy ending to this story. I am scared to die. What if the treatment does not work, and what if I die suddenly? There are no guarantees. Sometimes I feel like I can feel my body giving up. I never feel good anymore, and things are going to get harder before they get easier. Time is flying swiftly now, that precious time before the bone marrow transplant. I have become an emotional mess – crying at night because I am scared and being short with people for a reason I can only hope to know. I cannot talk about this to anyone because I do not find words to say. What is there to say? I do not feel good physically now – my ANC is 42, my platelets are low, and the treatment is taking its toll on my body more severely than ever before. I went to the clinic for a platelet transfusion on 7/27, and a red blood transfusion on 7/28. I had to go for an emergency platelet transfusion today because I was bleeding excessively from my period. It is the first time that has ever happened. It makes me feel like my body is giving up, and sometimes I feel that I am losing the hope I need to keep to get through this. The next two weeks are going to be a long, hard time to wait for bone marrow transplant. One of my biggest fears is that I will die in bone marrow transplant. There. I said it finally – the one thing that has been looming in my mind since the beginning of this treatment. Many other people have been through bone marrow transplant successfully. Will I make it? When did all the innocent young children and teenagers who lost their precious lives die? I do not know why my feelings have turned to a preoccupation with death lately and I do not know what happened to my positive attitude either. The night scares me. Darkness equals death – a cessation of life and the soul. The other thought that cannot help but periodically present itself in my mind is a feeling of guilt or shame or something of the sort. I am a person consumed with guilt for some reason, and it brings me down. What did I do wrong? Why did I get cancer? I tell everyone that it is not so bad. I say it is good that I got cancer because I have learned so much. What do I feel inside? I feel that I deserved to get cancer because I needed some humbling and some discipline to the reality of life. After the first treatment I forgot what it meant just to wake up breathing every day. What it meant to be able to walk around without having to sit every five minutes, for God's sake! What it meant to have a family that cares about me. Cancer brings me back to face these things. But do I cherish each day and try to live it to the fullest? No, I wake up irritable and hostile towards a world that has done nothing to me. My body – I – did it. My body and my mind failed, not the world. Sometimes my heart aches. Not physically, but I feel a pain inside that no pill, IV, anything can get rid of.

I cannot share that pain with anyone else (why burden them?), and yet sometimes I can barely cope with it alone. What if I go crazy and end it all someday? Then what? A whole life and lots of money wasted to save it, ending in death. Sometimes my guilt makes me feel like all this money and care is too much for my life, and it is not worth it. It seems crazy that one has to spend so much money to be tortured by the ills of chemotherapy and other unpleasant aspects of treatment. It is a paradoxical disease – feel a lot worse to feel better. Get as close to death as possible without dying. Is that why some people do not make it? One millimeter over the line and the treatment claims victory on a weakened body? Or cancer gets to make the claim if things go in the other direction. I got a big dose of Benadryl today with my platelets. It made me feel so inept that I was unable to speak or move my body. Paralyzed. Helpless. Sometimes I have out of body experiences where I see myself in whatever unpleasant situation I happen to be in. It is freaky. Is this normal? Maybe I am crazy!

## *Sad Sad Girl*

*Bloodshot eyes, shivering fear –*
*Could you shed even one more tear?*
*Such confusion, such lost dreams –*
*Life isn't always what it seems.*
*You once had a light that danced in your eyes –*
*Now you are pale, and weak, but wise.*
*You were carried off into a deep unknown –*
*I don't know where you went,*
*But I hope you went home.*

## Sunday, July 30, 2000

I do not feel better today. It seems like I never feel good anymore – physically or emotionally. I have sunken into a deep depression. Nothing matters anymore. I do not laugh easily and all my smiles are forced and fake. I am scared because I feel bad inside – like when I knew that the cancer had come back. Is there cancer lurking within my body still? Has something gone wrong or is something amiss? The doctors have told me that my sensitivity to what is happening in my body is amazing. Maybe it is, and at times I almost wish I did not have that knowledge. Maybe I am scared of all the tests coming up this week beginning tomorrow. What if they find something? Will that mean more of this living hell? Nobody could imagine this chaos that I feel inside. I hide it with my usual quiet demeanor, and try not to let any sign of this unpleasantness surface. Will I make myself more sick by keeping all this stress in? I worry about that. I never had this problem with severe depression last treatment. Sure there were the down times, but I never felt quite this bad. Maybe along with my body that is feeling exhausted and more defeated than victorious this time, my emotions have run rampant. The patient everyone sees is still happy Danielle who always has a smile and is so positive. It almost seems like you have to be happy and appear like treatment is not that bad. I don't want people to know how much it hurts me sometimes. They will worry and I do not want to cause that. On the other hand, you can't just act like this is not that bad, who cares? We will get through it. "We did it once, we'll do it again!" A phrase that makes me choke but sounds reassuring and positive to family and friends.

We will do it again – that is obvious, but will it be the last time? Maybe we will do it again, and again, and again until we find good health and a complete cure OR that other option that I have discussed at great length – the cancer and death claim the prize. What would the world do? How would people who always told me "It will be fine" feel? Perhaps choke on those words the next time they found themselves assuring someone else in a similar situation. I know I would. "I could not stop for death, so he kindly stopped for me," said Emily Dickinson. I could not hold the tears in today. They came flowing like a deluge as I crumpled to the floor against the cabinets after closing the bathroom door. I could not stop and yet I could not think of why I was crying. My chest heaved as I tried to keep from sobbing so that someone might hear and suspect. Another thing is my insomnia. When it is dark, I do not become tired. I read in the living room every night until two or three in the morning, when the lamp on the timer goes out. Then it is silence, dark, a feeling of death. I cannot stand the silence, so I reach to turn on the CD player. Carpenters. Christmas songs. They sound so happy and joyful. Perhaps somehow they can cheer me up. I stare wide-eyed in the dark. Numbness. Wake up to greet the next day with four or less hours of rest. WHY?? I almost wrote emails to people about the way I feel now. No, that would have been devastating! Don't tell everyone how you feel because treatment is going great and Danielle feels wonderful. I sometimes feel as if I am entering a catatonic state – I feel nothing, I see nothing, I hear nothing. Nothing matters. I stare off into never never land. Never die… While in my catatonic state I am focusing hard, concentrating. What is it that I think about? Is it in this world? I know not what. I think of nothing as my eyes stare into space. A vast space. Did I even tell about my platelet transfusion yesterday. My period was hemorrhaging and my platelets are only 24. And I am bruised all over. Just like a battered woman, but the person who is beating me is myself. My own body hurts itself. It cannot help it, when all its defenses are shot. All its own ammunition seized. All defenses down. Nobody can know about all this. My pain and my feelings are all my own and nobody can take them from me and I can't share them.

### *Fear of Night*

*Pop the pills quickly,*
*Make the pain go away.*
*Will I still be around,*
*To greet the new day?*
*My heart thumps awkwardly,*
*Within my chest.*
*I perspire nervously,*
*And cannot rest.*
*I cannot breathe –*
*I am dying.*
*As I crawl into bed,*
*I fall asleep crying.*
*Is that a lump in my neck?*
*Is the cancer back?*
*It is likely nothing,*
*But it is hope I lack.*
*Do I have a temp?*

*Is my pulse rate steady?*
*I cannot die –*
*I am not ready.*
*The room is spinning –*
*A dizzy spell.*
*My mind is touring*
*A senseless hell.*
*Will I make it?*
*I hope I will.*
*My mind is a chaos,*
*And I cannot be still.*
*One foot in the grave,*
*The other on its way.*
*This is the way*
*I end each day.*
*I hate to sleep,*
*I hate to think.*
*It feels like it's time,*
*And my hopes sink.*
*What if I die?*
*Will anyone care?*
*The saddest thing is*
*Nobody will be there.*
*I can't feel my body now.*
*I'm looking down at myself –*
*But how?*
*I hate the night –*
*It scares me to death;*
*And one of these lonesome nights,*
*I will take my last breath.*

## Monday, July 31, 2000

Well, here I am typing to you from the black lagoon. My mother calls me a mole person since I am always sitting in the dark. Anyway, I am writing to tell you about the events of day one for bone marrow approval. It was quite a day, and I find myself pretty exhausted just from going to the hospital to have tests done. First, we arrived in the oncology clinic and had to wait for quite some time, but that time was wonderful in retrospect because it was the only break there was in the whole day. The first event was a CBC that told us that my platelets are still low (not so low that I need a transfusion though, and it is not causing me problems right now), but my ANC is back up to 3000 which is a relief. That means that I do not have to have shots any more, which is always a welcome bit of news. We went down to radiology to receive my bone scan injection at 10am, which was quick. It was educational, as I questioned the woman about what was in the injection. It is an isotope of Technetium that bonds to the bones and joints, and becomes concentrated in areas where there is abnormal growth or tumors. This isotope has a half life of six hours, and the scan is done two hours after the injection. Therefore, the medicine is completely cleared out of the system in about twenty-four to thirty-six hours. So, that was my chemistry lesson of the day. I had to know because I like to know what they are putting in my body. After the bone scan injection, I went to get my chest and sinus X-Rays. That was alright, but the lady did not get it right the first time and had to do them all over again so it took a while longer. As soon as those were done, we had to rush upstairs, as we had been paged by the oncology clinic that the pulmonary doctor was waiting for us. So, we had the pulmonary consult, and were told the risks of bone marrow transplant on the lungs. The drugs and radiation can obviously bring about some problems, like pneumonia in some cases, but hopefully nothing too serious. And it is all treatable in various ways. Bone marrow transplant professionals are so meticulous that any problems that arise are dealt with promptly – preventing them from turning serious. After the pulmonary consult, the nurse came in with a bunch of stuff, and I knew it was not going to be pleasant. She had a hat and a jug – I have to collect all my liquid (if you know what I mean) for twenty-four hours. It is a major pain, but for some reason I guess they need it. I have yet to know why. We went down for my bone scan at 12pm, and that took an hour. I never enjoy those. It is an hour of being strapped to a table with weights on either side to prevent any movement. I was thankful that I was feeling well because that made the scan much easier. As soon as we finished the bone scan, I received a liter of contrast (barium) to drink for the CT scan. Then, we went back up to the clinic to wait and I drank the contrast and we saw some other people. I had my CT scan at 2pm, and it took a little over an hour. It was alright, but the lady was angry because the IV was not working well (or so she claims), and she could not push the injection in as quickly as she wanted to (everyone else seems to be able to push syringes of everything into my catheter just fine). The only bone to pick with the CT Scan is with the person who tells me when to hold my breath and when to breathe. Well, she said "Hold your breath" and like a minute passed. I was getting red in the face and about to pass out when the lady who was injecting noticed and said, "Oh, you can breathe now. I guess she forgot to tell you that you could." Okay. I was a little frustrated with that. The rest of the scan after that experience was alright. The final event of the day was drawing a bunch of blood for a litany of tests. The nurse drew 1/3 of a liter of blood and filled ten tubes with it. I have never had so much blood drawn, and I did feel a bit lightheaded, but did not pass out thank goodness. We will be having the same amount drawn tomorrow, as they could not draw all the tests today without causing some problems (they would have had to transfuse me if they drew more out). Well, that is about all that happened today. We are going back tomorrow but it does not have to be as early. Tomorrow is not as busy, I believe. I will write then about what we do.

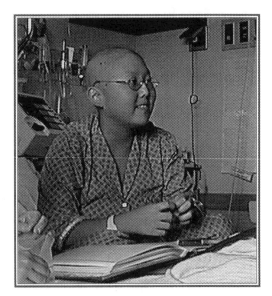

## Tuesday, August 1, 2000

I will not write as long as I am thoroughly exhausted from
the day's events. Unfortunately, as tired as my physical
body gets I still cannot sleep well, so become even more
tired. Anyway, on with the events! We walked into the
clinic this morning with my present (the 24-hour urine
collection) and delivered that to the BMT nurse. I had
my double height and weight taken, which is simply that
– taking height and weight two times to make damn sure
that the chemotherapy and all the other medications are
given in very accurate amounts. We had a consultation
with the BMT coordinator, and she went over different
aspects of the experience, what to expect, how to clean
the house, etc. After that we went to the bone marrow
transplant unit for a tour. It was good to see the place
where I will spend such a long time. Actually, the unit was
very nice, as far as a hospital can go. There are only six
rooms in BMT, and the environment is very, very strict.
Everybody must wear gowns, and a different gown must
be worn for being in my room, and being in the general
hall of BMT. I will have to wear a mask everywhere I
go in order to protect from dust and other things in the
air. There is a litany of do's and don'ts. The tour was very
thorough and I know what to expect now with BMT
as far as surroundings. Unfortunately, I could not take
in everything about the unit because I felt like doubling
over in pain from the antibiotics that I have been taking.
The good thing is that today was the last day. After BMT,
we went to the cardiology clinic for the echocardiogram.
I certainly had more in store than I knew. In addition
to the echocardiogram, there was also an EKG, and the

exercise EKG. That was certainly a surprise. Basically, the people told me, "We are going to make you run on a treadmill until you feel you are ready to die, and then we will make you run more." I began at a walking pace, and every three minutes the treadmill inclined more, and doubled speed. My absolute maximum heart rate is 203. They wanted at least 85% of that. I felt like I was going to die, and she said just two more minutes. I got my heart rate up to 193, so we were pretty close. They rushed me off the treadmill and flopped me sideways on a table to jab me in the ribs and heart to record everything. Needless to say it was not too pleasant. Now I see why the nurse said to make sure and eat lunch (which I didn't), and the doctor asked if the shoes I was wearing would work for a treadmill (they would have been fine for a walk but they were heavy Doc Martens and therefore not ideal for running top speed!). After that, we went back up to the oncology clinic to meet with the BMT doctor who is taking care of me. He examined me, and said that all my tests are good so far. There was no sign of the cancer or anything bad on all the X-Rays and scans, thank God. The only thing that is abnormal so far is that I do not have the regular amount of antibodies, but the doctor said that my numbers were typical of someone who has undergone chemotherapy treatment. If they go too low all that will happen is I will have something like a transfusion to infuse some antibodies. Not a big deal. That was all the events for today. Tomorrow is my big day when they will draw another 1/3 liter of blood for more tests, and I have a bone marrow aspirate and the spinal tap. They have decided to inject more chemotherapy into the spinal tap just to be on the safe side. I'll let you know how it all goes. Sorry I am sort of grumpy tonight. I guess you can probably tell. This is one week when I will be very glad to see Friday come.

## Saturday, August 5, 2000

I have just finished my bone marrow transplant workup week, which was super busy! Other than my hips still hurting from the bone marrow aspirates, I seem pretty unscathed and there are no traumatic signs of this busy week:

7/31: Met with the transplant coordinator regarding workup cultures, had the pulmonary consult, bone scan, chest and sinus x-rays, CT scans of neck, chest and abdomen.

8/1: Met with the nurse practitioner for patient/parent education, bone marrow transplant unit tour, EKGs and stress echocardiograms

8/2: Dental consult, lab tests, bone marrow biopsy, lumbar puncture (spinal tap), history and physical with bone marrow transplant doctor

8/3: Audiogram, pulmonary function tests, dietary consult and signing consents

So, that was my schedule and it was busy!

## Sunday, August 6, 2000 2:45am

The reason I am not asleep now and not at all tired is because I took a LONG nap today. I was not feeling well the whole day due to a new medication, and so decided to sleep it off. I went to sleep around 2pm and did not wake up until 7pm! The evening was just beginning for me around 10pm, and it is apparently not over yet. I just hope that my parents do not wake up and find me out here in the living room on my computer. I don't think that they would be happy about that. I have decided that this last week before transplant there is no time. I can stay up as late as I want and wake up whenever I want. After all, I gotta live a little on the wild side! I feel sort of silly but then I think about all the rules that I will have to follow, and all the time that I will be stuck in that hospital room, and I do not think that it is so crazy. Oh, I forgot to tell you WHY I am stuck with a new medication in the week that was supposed to be fun and med-free. The audiology clinic called yesterday to let us know that while I was waiting for my audiogram, I was exposed to chicken pox. Isn't that wonderful? We informed them that I was immuno-suppressed and they did nothing about it, and I was exposed to the chicken pox. The doctor is expecting, and we are hoping, that my high titer level will keep me from getting the virus. The med I am on is Acyclovir. Although it will not prevent me from getting symptoms, it will lessen the effects if I do get symptoms. The worst part of it all that my mother calls inexcusable, is that the audiology clinic is saying that we lied, and never told them I was at risk. They told the oncology clinic that we lied when the oncology clinic called to complain. Can you believe that?!? It has been nice weather here, although a little on the warm side. I haven't been getting out too much because it is pretty hot, and I haven't felt that good. I am planning on going to the farmer's market tomorrow, I mean today. The dietitian came in to talk to us the other day, and she said that she is the one in charge of all the IV nutrition, and that the doctors and nurses do whatever she tells them. I told her that I want to lose a few pounds in the course of events, and she said that she could arrange that. She said that most people come out of the bone marrow transplant unit at the same weight they went in, which surprised me. I have always thought of people going through bone marrow transplant and becoming sickly and emaciated. She said that we can go on the low end of my caloric requirements when I am on hyperalimentation so that I can come out of the unit a few pounds lighter. That makes me happy as you can imagine. We watched a wonderful movie tonight. It was called "Little Voice" and it is about a young girl who can imitate the voices of stars such as Judy Garland and Ella Fitzgerald. Well, the light on the timer is about to go out in the living room (at 3am here). I do not want to be in the dark. I am having a Carpenters marathon in my room – listening to all the songs they ever recorded. So I will go back to that. Talk to you soon!

## Monday, August 14, 2000 2:37am

It is another one of those sleepless nights. Nothing is happening. The minutes seem to be ticking away at lightning speed on the digital clock. I am listening to the radio. They play all kinds of songs that I have never heard at night. That must be when they play the ones that people do not like. I do not know why I cannot sleep. I was pretty tired earlier. I am really out of it. I cannot talk about anything – writing is the only way I can discuss anything that I am feeling. I am really happy that I am able to write poetry again – I have been waiting for the time when I would be in that mood again. Well, I guess that I will try to sleep again. Sorry to write this really boring journal that probably does not make any sense owing to the time of day.

## *Misconceptions*

*Why can nobody understand?*
*Because they cannot begin to know how.*
*Maybe they will know in the future,*
*What I'm experiencing now.*
*They think that they know everything –*
*Every feeling and every thought;*
*But the truth is only my own,*
*And has never been sought.*
*Nobody knows the secret fear,*
*And discomfort of every night.*
*Each thought and feeling a worrisome sign,*
*That something is not right.*
*I do not know how to cope, or wait –*
*Will I ever be normal again?*
*Perhaps the answer lies in the future –*
*But it may not matter by then.*

## Tuesday, August 15, 2000 Transplant Experience #1

Today was check-in day for the beginning of my bone marrow transplant experience. I had somewhat of an unpleasant surprise though. This morning when I checked into the clinic in order to get the okay from my doctor that I was ready to begin, he told me that I was expected in radiology for a CT scan of my sinuses. One of my pulmonary culture tests was not normal, and contained traces of an infection called Aspergillus. It is the most serious fungus that can attack the sinuses, and needs immediate treatment if it begins to grow out of control. My sinus CT scan was not normal, in that the sinus that is furthest back (behind the eye) on my left side is half to three quarters filled with fluid. This is not normal for anyone. This fluid may be caused by something else, or it may be the Aspergillus developing. Either way, I cannot proceed with transplant until we know. So, tomorrow I will be having surgery to drain the fluid from the sinus (as it is completely clogged), and to find out whether the infection is a concern. I have been feeling fine otherwise, so this is the only way to truly know. The surgery is fairly short – one and a half to two hours. I will be under general anesthesia, and the surgery is scheduled for 5pm. However, the doctors are going to try as hard as possible to fit me in sooner. It could take one to two days to recover from the surgery, but then I should be feeling alright. If it is not the Aspergillus virus, then I will probably begin my transplant chemotherapy on Saturday or Sunday. However, if it is Aspergillus, the infection must be treated aggressively and for a long period of time, and transplant would be delayed for a month. This means that I would need to have another course of chemotherapy to compensate for the chemotherapy that was supposed to begin tomorrow. The reason that the transplant must be postponed is because the chemotherapy wipes out my immune system completely, and I would not have the necessary cells to fight anything this serious if I had the chemotherapy and the infection became out of control. We were told today that the chemotherapy is so strong and depresses the immune system to such an extent that former viruses, such as the chicken pox, which have antibodies within the body, can reconstitute themselves and become illness again. About 50% of the patients experience recurrent chicken pox in the form of shingles following transplant. However, I have many medications that attempt to prevent every possible scenario. So, that is the biggest news of today. I will probably be in the bone marrow transplant unit for four weeks, depending on whether I stay here.

## Wednesday, August 16, 2000 11:05 PM Transplant Experience #2

The update for today will not be as detailed, as I am still recovering from the surgery. However, everything went very well, and it looks as if there will be little concern for the sinus CT scan, and that it is most likely not the Aspergillus fungus. Also, the ENT doctor discovered that there was not any fluid to be found in the sinus – I do not quite understand this, as I do not know what else could cause the area to be shaded in my sinus on the X-Ray. I will have to ask. So, they took a scraping of the area just to make absolutely certain, and will do some tests on that. Anyway, I do not have any bruising from the surgery, and my nose did not bleed that much. The bruising would have occurred if they had a difficult time reaching the location of the sinus, and had to deal with going through the bone or cartilage. Fortunately, that did not happen. I had a headache and was a bit tired when I first came out of day surgery, but otherwise, I was fine. I do have quite a sore throat due to the tube that was placed there during the operation, but it should be improved by tomorrow. Tomorrow is my "day of rest," and they are still planning on going ahead with the transplant later this week unless there is a shocking revelation between now and Friday. I will be starting the heavy-dose chemotherapy for transplant on Friday, and that will be day -8. Each day is counted down from day -8, and the only difference with me is that I will have had three day -8's! Day -8 is preparation, and then chemotherapy begins on day -7 until day -1. Day 0 is transplant day, when I will get my cells back. So, this is the plan right now. They have put me on many medicines now, which does not make me too happy. I have some extra pills here, and mouthcare to prevent infections and discomforts. Well, I will write again tomorrow! They are letting me out again tomorrow night for a dinner pass. That means that I can leave the hospital with my parents to have a decent dinner, rather than this hideous hospital food. I am so happy that I can do that one last time. They would have let me out tonight, but I was not really up to it quite yet.

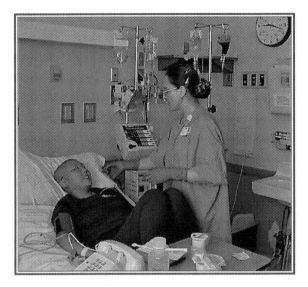

## Thursday, August 17, 2000 10:59 PM Transplant Experience #3

Not much happened today, but I did have the privilege of taking two passes out of the unit to have a decent lunch and dinner with my family. It is always so special and wonderful to escape this place, and we had a nice time. I made a deal with the nurse that I would drink plenty of fluids on my own today, and therefore managed to stay disconnected from the IV fluids. It was nice to not have to drag my tall, skinny friend everywhere that I went. I was introduced to a couple more unpleasant medicines today, one being the nasal spray that will fight any infections, such as the Aspergillus, that may be lingering. I am feeling quite well from the surgery. The only issues are occasional headaches, and still a bit of an irritated throat. Otherwise, recovery seems to be progressing quite well. The chemotherapy for the transplant will begin tomorrow.

I will have seven days of continuous chemotherapy, and then a day of rest before the transplant. I am going to be the first patient in six years that has had a transplant on the weekend! The hospital does not often do weekend transplants since none of the technicians or anyone is regularly here then. Well, that is about all that happened today. I do not know when I will next be able to write, but you can be sure that I will write as soon as possible.

## Sunday, August 27, 2000 Transplant Email

I am very happy to write and say that I have had a successful autologous bone marrow transplant! My transplant took place on August 26, 2000, and was quite an eventful happening despite prior expectations. In the times leading up to the transplant, seemingly every person told me that the transplant is a very anticlimactic happening in contrast to the intensive preparation preceding it. I was not disappointed with an uneventful day that was "just like any other red blood transfusion" as I had been told many times and come to expect. Rather, the day held quite a bit of excitement for me and the team taking care of me. My first bag of cells began to infuse at 9am, and seemed quite uneventful. The second bag was thawed, and halfway through this bag is when the excitement began. I began to experience difficulty breathing, I became very hot, and my blood pressure skyrocketed. I was immediately given more Benadryl, hydrocortisone, and some medication to lower my blood pressure. Although the reactions were quite severe, the doctors said that they were not as bad as they could be, and that the cells must be given in the correct allotment of time, or they would not be effective. By that point, I was not very conscious, and quite worried, but the third bag of cells was given, and I was soon given about two hours of rest before the next infusion of cells. In this time, I was able to recover somewhat. I began to dread the second infusion because the doctor said that usually the reaction is worse the second time as compared to the first. Understandably, this idea rattled me a bit, but the second time we were also better prepared for the reaction that we had not known would happen the first time. I was premedicated heavily, and my symptoms were not nearly as severe. These reactions were caused by the preservative that enables the blood cells to be frozen, called DMSO, and also by the great amount of fluid that is being pushed into the system. Therefore, I had my successful bone marrow transplant! I did not feel too well for the remainder of the day, but began to feel very well by last night. Today, August 27, I am feeling quite well, although a bit wearied from all the events. The doctors said that they would be thrilled if my stem cells graft within two and a half weeks to three, but this would be quite quickly. When my cells graft, they will begin to establish themselves within the bone marrow and multiply, and this process happens more quickly with autologous transplants (own cells) as opposed to those where a donor's cells are used. The amount of time that I will be in the hospital all depends upon my cells, and how quickly my immune system recovers. Although the healthy cells are in my system, my blood counts will continue to decrease now from the high-dose chemotherapy that I had, until the new cells establish themselves.

## Saturday, September 2, 2000 9:17 AM

I feel really pooped today, but that does not mean that I will let myself get away with not getting on the treadmill! I still plan to do my exercise. I got a red transfusion this morning, and have had two or three platelet transfusions so far. I will probably need one again by later today or tomorrow. My dad is coming today, and my mom is going to stay at the house for awhile to clean some things. Yesterday the nurse came in to begin discussion of discharge, so that was an exciting thought! She said typically they might start seeing a change in my white count at day +10 – maybe on Monday. It has been at .1 for awhile now. She said not to be worried if the cells do not begin to graft by then. When my counts start going up, I will get passes to leave the hospital. Anywhere but my house, or Charlie's house, I will have to wear a mask for three months! I guess that is not too great a price for freedom…

## Tuesday, September 5, 2000 6:11 PM

It has been a bit hectic lately with some new problems that have arisen. I have been having some chest pains when I breathe, and had an X-Ray taken just the other day. Today, I had a follow-up X-Ray taken, and a smudge appeared in the area where my pain is. Therefore, I am having a CT Scan done this evening to determine if there is anything of concern. Meanwhile, I have finally been put in isolation, which means that all the nurses wear masks, gloves, and gowns when they come into my room. I cannot leave my room any longer, except for medical procedures or tests. I have not been leaving it as of late anyway, as I have not been feeling very well. I feel as if I am poison or something that they should not be around! I suppose that I will get used to it. Previous to these new happenings, everything has gone rather well, and I have been feeling alright. I had been exercising on the treadmill, and been up and about a bit. My appetite has been good, although I have had a bit of stomach upset lately. I had been having troubles sleeping, and I have finally found a wonderful sleeping pill that has solved my problems. It is called Trazadone, and it enables me to first fall asleep, and then resume sleep when I am woken up during the night. It is wonderful. The transplant has been a success, and my cells have begun to graft, which means that they are beginning to work in my bone marrow. My white count remained at .1 for some time, and then it began to recover. Today, I am at an ANC of over 800! I need an ANC of 1000 to leave. This morning, the doctors had said that I might be leaving the hospital by the beginning of next week, but with these new developments, we are not sure. We just hope that this is nothing serious, and that it will pass. I will let you know what happens. If nothing serious is discovered tonight, I will have a pass tomorrow, which means that I will be able to leave the hospital for a few hours to go home, or for a walk, or for a drive. It will be wonderful if I can get out of here for a few hours.

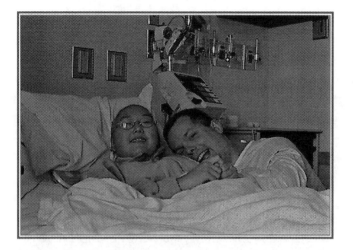

## Tuesday, September 5, 2000 10:05 PM

As promised, I had a CT scan this evening to confirm suspicions of the pains in my chest. There is indeed a culprit that is the cause of the pain. I have a lesion on my left lung, that is somewhat in the shape of a triangle. The broader side of the triangle is on the outside of my lung, and the smaller side is within the lung. The lesion is irritating the pleurae, which are the sacs surrounding the lungs. That is the cause of the pleurisy-type pains that I experience when inhaling. Most likely, the cause of the lesion is a fungal infection in the lung, and much less likely, a tumor. The doctor has no reason to believe that it is caused by a bacterial infection, because he says that I look too well, and that I would be feeling very sick and coughing a great deal. The most likely solution is to go in to surgery to remove the lesion. In fact, I am NPO (no food or drink) from 6am on tomorrow, in case they decide to go into the operating room to solve this then.

The doctor will talk to the surgeon tomorrow morning, to see what this procedure would involve. If it is very risky, then I will be treated with antibiotics to see if those cure the infection. However, if it is not very risky, they would like to go into surgery within the next 48 hours. So, as my mother says, this is like turbulence on an airplane. I say that it is another bump in the road. Either way, it is another procedure that will soon be a memory. Other than that, there are not many new happenings. I had two outings from the bone marrow transplant unit today. Maybe not where I would have chosen to go, but it was time out of my room, especially now that I have been put in isolation. I will probably receive another platelet transfusion (the blood-clotting factor) tomorrow as they are border-line today.

## Wednesday, September 6, 2000 12:59 PM

Here is the latest scoop on what is happening. Today, the doctor came in and reiterated his belief that this is a fungal infection that is attacking my lung. He also mentioned that he noticed a couple of dark spots in my right lung yesterday during the CT scan. He is not sure what those are yet. It is just another one of those bumps in the road. I will have some scans today, as they are trying to decide about imaging and other considerations for the surgery. I will definitely be having a sinus scan, but I am unsure of what else may lie in store for me today. I suppose that the sinus scan is to see what progress the amphotericin nasal spray has had on my aspergillus colonization in the sinus. The surgery is tentatively scheduled for 5:15pm tomorrow evening, and I do not know how long it takes or what it involves. Everyone who has come into my room this morning has asked me if I am worried about the surgery. I have to say that I am not that worried, as I have had so many surgeries already. This surgery will be a somewhat more major affair than anything that I have had. My other surgeries have been rather superficial, just biopsies and placements. I know that this will not be a piece of cake, but at least it will alleviate the pain (in the long run!) and will solve the mystery of what is in there. My dose of morphine has been increased, as the pain has become a bit worse. It does truly help me, as well as the other medications. I am no longer NPO (no food or drink) since they are not doing the surgery today! That is some good news, because I have been longing for a drink of water. I have been feeling pretty tired, but I am still able to eat and drink. My ANC is over 1,000 today, so there is some good news to conclude this message. I should be out of here as soon as these issues are cleared up. By the way, if this is a fungal infection, it is very treatable. I will just have to stay in the hospital long-term to receive a very strong antibiotic called Ambisome. It will be worth it if it gets rid of this nasty stuff though!

## Thursday, September 7, 2000 1:02 PM

This will be short, as I am rather dizzy and sick from the morphine and the unpleasant drug that I was given last night. Unfortunately, last night was an exciting night (which is not good in hospitals!). It all began with this drug called IVIG (Intravenous Immunoglobulin) that boosts one's immune system. It is somewhat like a blood transfusion, but I do not believe that people donate it – it is made synthetically. It is a natural part of the body's defense system, and it should be at 500 or above. Mine was at 470, so I was just below what I needed. The infusion went over three hours, and mine was started very slowly in an attempt to avoid the severe reactions that the medicine can cause. I did not have a reaction in the beginning, so the nurse increased the infusion rate. I did not notice anything at first, but then the excitement began. I began to get chills up and down my back (I could not get warm with six blankets!), and my teeth were chattering. I had chest pains from my lung condition, and then my fever spiked. I had a temperature of 39.5C, which is around 103.1F. I was feeling really badly, and either the morphine or the IVIG made me very emotionally unstable, so I was not able to take anything well. Fortunately, after about an hour, having had all the medications began to make me feel better, I began to feel alright again. I was able to eat dinner, enjoy a video, take my evening medications, and then my sleeping pill for a sound night's rest. The other events of yesterday were two CT scans – one of my sinuses, and the other of my head. The doctor said that the good news is that I have a brain! He said that there was nothing in the head scan, and in the sinus scan I still have fluid in the same sinus that they performed the surgery on. It is alright though, as I am already on medicine for it. Last night, my chest pain seemed to have worsened, so I was started on a new system for administering my pain medicine, which is morphine. I have a special pump called a PCA. It is rather nifty, as it constantly administers small amounts of the medicine – 2mg/hour. If I have more pain that requires more relief, I press a button, and it gives me extra medicine. The button can be pressed every ten minutes, but I have not had to use it that much. It is programmed so that I cannot accidentally overdose. I cannot exceed 6mg/4 hours. I think this is a wonderful contraption, and it has really helped my pain because I do not have to wait for the nurse to come. This morning I had another chest X-Ray in preparation for the surgery. Nobody has told us about it yet. I am getting more platelets later this morning because my count is low again, and I am going into surgery. Later in the afternoon (nobody knows when), the surgeon will come talk to us about the procedure, what is involved, risks, etc. I have had this surgeon before for other surgeries, which is always nice. Well, I need to sign off now. The surgery is scheduled for 5:15pm tonight. I am NPO (nothing by mouth) all day, but it does not bother me because I am not feeling like anything anyway.

## Thursday, September 7, 2000 3:10pm

I had another CT scan this afternoon, and the surgery is still definitely a go for tonight. Granted, the surgeon has not come to discuss anything with us yet, but I certainly hope that he will before the surgery. Treatment for a fungal infection within the lungs with Ambisome can range anywhere from two weeks to six months in the hospital. The doctor tends to think that I would be on the shorter end of the spectrum, but it remains to be seen if this is indeed a fungal infection. This procedure is common and easy to all the doctors here. Many patients go through it. So, that is all the news for now.

## Thursday, September 7, 2000 4:28 PM

I am back to provide up to the minute coverage of the happenings here (just like the news!) I am itching all over, which would imply a reaction to the second batch of platelets that I got later this afternoon. More Benadryl to knock the reaction and me out! The other excitement that is happening now is that my catheter appears to be clotted, and will not draw or flush. They are trying to fix it. As if this were not exciting enough in itself, it is also a little under an hour before surgery now! I am having surgery with fluoroscopy, and the procedure will take one and a half to two hours. I will be under general anesthetic, and may require a breathing tube, a chest tube, and oxygen after. And of course increased pain medicine – the morphine. People have told me most patients begin to feel better when the chest tube is removed. The procedure sounds like it has been done many times, and that it is easy for the doctors and surgeons. Easy for them at least…..

## Saturday, September 9, 2000 4:46 PM

This message will be shorter as I still have a fair amount of pain from the surgery, and cannot use the left side of my body for anything because it hurts. The surgery on Thursday night went very well, and was not too difficult for the surgeon. It went quickly, about an hour and a half, and the incisions that they made in my side were not too big. I have a chest tube stuck in my left side to drain the fluids and blood from the surgery, and it makes breathing painful because it is placed between my lung and the chest wall, and every time I move or breathe, it rubs. The tube was supposed to have come out yesterday, Friday, but I had an unpleasant happening yesterday. The pain after the surgery on Thursday night was severe, and no amount of morphine seemed to improve the pain. I could barely breathe because my chest hurt so much. Friday morning, things were not getting any better, so they increased the dose of morphine from 2.5mg/hr to 3.5mg/hr. It still did not help the pain. My mother went down for lunch, and by the time that she came back up, I was beginning to have serious problems. I could barely breathe, and kept fading in and out of consciousness. When my mother and the nurse were asking me what was wrong, I said that it was hard to get a breath, and that my heart hurt. When my mother asked another question, and I could not answer, we all became scared. This had all come on after a guy came in to do the X-Ray. Unable to move on my own, the guy shoved me upward, and then pushed me hard on the side where my chest tube is. It took my breath away, and I had a difficult time getting it back. The X-ray person left, and then I could not breathe. The doctor came rushing in, listened, and then I cannot remember exactly what happened, I sort of went into shock. I could not breathe, and the pressure on my heart was so great it felt as if it had stopped beating. I had pulmonary edema, and my lungs were so filled with fluid that they were pressing on my heart. The emergency medical team came rushing into my room, along with many of the oncology nurses, and there must have been about 25 people in the room.

I felt my body beginning to shut down, and almost lost the image of life completely when suddenly I came to again. The nurses were desperately pumping syringes of different medicines into my IV, and everyone was yelling different requests to one another. I was very scared, and thought that I was not going to live. Then, suddenly, I heard the doctor say that I had come back to them, or that they had succeeded in reviving me. It gave me new hope, and I tried harder to breathe than before. It was a struggle for me to keep my eyes open, and to keep breathing. The social worker was by my side the whole time, reminding me to breathe. I remember thinking that this was the first time in my life that I had had to think about breathing, making it a voluntary action. The cause of my problems was the fluid in my lungs, coupled with the high amount of morphine that I had in my system. Morphine makes breathing less frequent, and also more shallow. Between the overwhelming amount of fluid and the morphine, my system began to shut down. Thanks to the fast work of Dr. F. and the emergency medical team, my life was saved. I have a foley catheter that was placed again to collect all the fluid that was escaping my system. I do not mind as much this time since it is so painful to move. I was given a medicine called Lasix, that is a diuretic, and released some of the fluid from my lungs. The other medicine that saved my life was Narcan, that reversed the effects of the morphine, and cleansed my system of it. I was given a great deal of Narcan, which kept me present in this world. This was a very scary experience for me, and one that I will never forget. I am having another chest x-ray done this afternoon to see how much fluid is still in my lungs. If it is good enough, they will take the chest tube out this afternoon. Otherwise, they will leave it in. I will be much more comfortable once it is removed. My counts are still going up, which is great. The other news is that I have a fungus in my lungs. They need to find out what kind and how to treat it. Well, that is the news from here. I need to go because I am beginning to have trouble seeing because I am so tired.

## _Looking Fear In the Face_

_A tranquil afternoon,_
_When all is going well –_
_And then it happens._
_Struggling for a single breath,_
_Of precious replenishing air._
_My heart aches, literally, as it thumps awkwardly within me._
_Chest heaves, as I struggle to survive –_
_The doctor rushes in._
_A look of panic._
_All becomes black._
_I'm in, and then I'm out again._
_I awake to find myself covered in perspiration –_
_Oxygen blasting in my face._
_So many people with syringes,_
_The doctor constantly checking my pulse –_
_God I feel awful._
_I think I ask what is happening to me,_
_But maybe that was only in my mind;_
_Because the emergency team is occupied –_
_And no one answers._
_So this is what it is like –_

*The end.*
*Then I come back, and regain hope —*
*The doctor relaxes.*
*I've returned.*
*Excruciating pain…*
*It pains me to breathe,*
*But I know it's the only way to survive.*
*I must breathe —*
*Breathe in, two, three,*
*And breathe out, two, three…to survive.*
*It was suddenly bright —*
*In the place I went, when I left,*
*But Grandma told me to go back —*
*And to stay alive.*
*Slowly but surely,*
*The morphine and Narcan wear off.*
*Fluids flow out of me quickly,*
*And I can breathe again.*
*Although the pain in my chest is severe,*
*I know it is a good pain —*
*It is the pain of life.*
*Everyone has left —*
*Save a few.*
*I am washed clean;*
*Clean of the perspiration and struggle,*
*That dirtied my body;*
*But also washed clean of the darkness of death.*
*Never have I been so afraid,*
*And never will I take another breath for granted.*

## Sunday, September 10, 2000 2:40 PM

This will be short, as I seem to become rather exhausted from typing on the computer. I think it is all the drugs, along with the discomfort of this chest tube. Well, last night was not calm and relaxing, as we had been hoping this weekend would be. It all began in the afternoon, when I was given some Benadryl for itching that the morphine has been causing. I had been drowsy all day, and the Benadryl knocked me into a deep sleep. This was abnormal, as Benadryl never has any effect on me any more. I slept until about 6:30pm, when I woke up to find an unpleasant tightness in my chest. It was not painful to breathe, but it was difficult. Sure enough, the same procedure that had taken place on Friday was followed yesterday, but on a much smaller scale. I was given Lasix and Narcan, and the morphine was reversed. I had to face the same scary effects of coming out of the influence of a strong narcotic again. I felt shivering cold, it was difficult to remember to breathe, and I felt as if I could fade out of the picture anytime. I began to get sick, and cough up a lot of phlegm and blood (which was very good because that was what was preventing me from breathing well). I begin to feel as if I cannot respond to anyone when I am in that state, although people ask me many questions. I break out in a cold sweat, and feel as if I am not quite present in the room. Fortunately, the feeling passed, and by the late evening I was back to normal again (as normal as you can be with a lot of tubes sticking out). It is scary until I reach that point though. My morphine dose is down even more now, and hopefully I will be able to get my chest tube out today, which would mean the morphine would stop too. I will probably stay on oxygen overnight, just to be safe. Well, I need to go now. I will write again when I next feel that I can. I hope that I do not have anything exciting to tell you.

## Tuesday, September 12, 2000 7:12 PM

I am writing to let you know that I am doing fairly well again. I have spent these past few days recovering from my eventful weekend. Friday was the scariest experience by far, and one that I will never forget. Being in such a dangerous place really made me realize what is important in life, and made me realize that I need to pay more attention to my needs and what is good for me. The main bone marrow transplant doctor came in last night, and said that he had heard about my "fireworks" over the weekend. I suppose that one could call not breathing some fireworks. He also said that I have paid more than my dues in this hospital stay. On Saturday, unfortunately, I had to go through the same experience as Friday again, but not nearly as seriously. I began to have difficulty breathing again, so the nurses reversed the morphine with the same drug, Narcan, and it fixed everything, but gave me the same terrible sensations that I had experienced the day before. Needless to say, I was positively exhausted by Sunday, and just lay in bed all day. I was still recovering Monday, and today it seems that I have made somewhat of a turnaround. I am terrified of the narcotic drugs, and also of the Narcan for the terrible way that it makes me feel. The pain from my surgery is still there, but not nearly as noticeable. On Sunday, I had my chest tube removed, which made breathing much less painful, and movement much easier. I also had the foley catheter removed, which made me all the more comfortable. I am not sure if I told you about what the surgery involved, but a small part of my left lung was removed, as there was a nodule between my chest wall and the lung that was causing great pain for me with breathing, as it was disturbing the pleural sacs and lining that surround the lung. In doing the surgery, the pain was much worse initially, but I knew that in the long run it would improve everything, and it has. After Friday's episode, we had discovered that there was a lot of extra fluid in my lungs, that caused the pulmonary edema then. That fluid has slowly been coming out over the past few days, and my lungs are finally sounding clear again. I have been receiving the kinds of treatments that patients with cystic fibrosis receive, in order to clear my lungs of anything else. I do not want any fluid in my lungs, as that can easily lead to pneumonia, or some other unwanted complication. My treatments consist of a Ventolin inhaler, that asthmatics use, followed by a ten or fifteen minute nebulizer treatment, where I simply breathe in a medication. That happens twice a day, and will end tonight since I am sounding so clear. The fungus within my lungs will take a long time to treat, but it is treatable. I have been receiving the IV treatments of Ambisome in the hospital, and will continue to receive them at home when I leave the hospital. It could take a couple of months to completely cure it. The doctors said that they are not too concerned about fungal infections because I am on so many medications, and also they said that I have the worst one that I could contract already

– the aspergillus fungus. The big news of today is that I had my first pass out of the hospital! The objective of passes is to prepare the patient for discharge, so that it is not a big shock in the excitement of everything. It gives the patient a chance to get used to wearing the protective mask everywhere, and to get used to moving around again. I had a three hour pass. We dropped by Starbucks to get one of my favorite drinks, and then went to Charlie's house where we will be staying until I can go home after discharge. We had dinner, and then it was time to come back here. I saved the best news for last! The doctor said today that it looks as if I can be discharged on Thursday, as long as everything goes well until then. Only one more day here!!! It seems so amazing, as things seemed to have taken such a down turn last week, and this week, they are completely the opposite. I will have to come to the hospital almost every day the first week after leaving, but at least I will not have to stay here. I am so happy. Today marks exactly one month from the day of my admission. So, although it was not a very long stay, it was certainly filled with its moments. The staff throws a party for every patient on discharge day, so I am excited for that, and to begin living a semi-normal life again. So, that is all the news from here. I am glad that I can write and give you some good news now. I will write again soon!

## September 12, 2000 7:57 PM

My first pass out today was wonderful. As planned, we stopped by Starbucks to pick up one of my favorite drinks, and then we went Christian's to hang out and relax. I was amazed at how tired I was, but I enjoyed getting out so much. We had dinner, and then it was time to go back to the hospital. My nurse said that I looked so happy and good when I came back, and that she was so glad I had that pass. I was too!

## September 17, 2000 7:30 PM

I am writing to let you know that I have officially been discharged from the bone marrow transplant unit! I am sorry that I have not written sooner – I have been free since Thursday, and everything has been going well since then. I have been pretty exhausted recovering from my stay, and also adjusting to home life again. I am staying at Charlie's house in Denver, which has been very convenient. It feels safe to be so close to the hospital, and is much less of an ordeal than the trip from Fort Collins in case of a surprise visit. The nurses and staff threw me a little party on Thursday, which was wonderful. I was given cake and a few presents, and some of the nurses who had taken care of me came in to give me their best wishes. It was such a happy day. I have been receiving IV medication at home through the homecare service, and also have frequent clinic visits to check blood counts and other concerns. I expect that I will be in Denver at least another month, as I have radiation treatment yet to come, and that will take at least two weeks in itself. I will keep you updated, but will hopefully not have as much news from now on.

## Friday, September 29, 2000

Today was the second checkup at the oncology clinic for this week. It held the dreaded anticipation of the pulmonary functions tests, but on the other hand, it is always comforting for me to know that nothing is going seriously wrong in my system. It was actually not as bad as I had remembered. Perhaps it was better this time since I came knowing what to expect. The unknown is always the scariest experience. It seems strange that to test the functions of the lungs, one must be pushed to the point where they feel like passing out. In the oncology clinic following pulmonary, my blood counts were checked, as well as potassium levels. Since the medicine for the lung infection decreases the potassium, I had my supplement increased. It seems amazing that in treatment, almost everything that is done must be counteracted or reversed before it causes another issue. Or another situation is that a medicine will not work if it is not given in conjunction with another. As with cancer treatment in general, it seems strange and paradoxical. My doctor says having a cancer diagnosis is being caught between a rock and a hard place. Sometimes the thought of living for me with the chance of becoming ill again is difficult, but on the other hand, the thought of death is scary too. I was exhausted today, with no energy whatsoever. It does not feel right not to accomplish much in a day, and yet so much is being accomplished in my immune system and recovery. However, it seems like a silent accomplishment since it is one that nobody sees, and one that I cannot feel. Sometimes it seems like an eternity to feel good again, but this is a very well-tread path for me, and I know that things will eventually improve, and life will be good again.

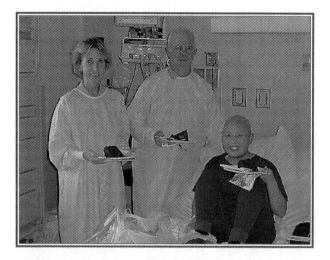

## September 30, 2000

I worked on school work today. I read "The Lottery" by Shirley Jackson, and was quite surprised by the turn of events that takes place within the story. I was puzzled throughout the whole story as to what "the lottery" was, and then shocked to have the true cause of the lottery revealed. The ending seemed somewhat disturbing, and I was still a bit confused as to why the people of the town performed this ritual. I saw the character who was stoned as a scapegoat, perhaps a sacrifice to keep evil away from the town. I gathered that the characters were superstitious, and perhaps this was the reason for the annual ritual. Although the woman who is chosen is not a likable character (and I believe the author planned it that way), it is still surprising to see what happens to her. Another thought that came to mind for me while reading the story, and seeing the transformation in the woman who is chosen, is that many people are mere facades. The lady was all sweetness and enthusiasm about the ritual day until she realized that her family, and maybe even herself, were in danger. Some people will go only so far with sacrifice and kindness, and once they are in trouble, they do not care about anyone else. Only what they need and want. The story struck me as rather bizarre, yet it was very interesting. The unique idea and way in which the story was written sets it apart from most literary works I've read. This seemed to be a successful short story, since it included a conflict, strong description, and a hook to interest the reader in continuing. The last theme that came to mind for me in reading the story is revenge. At the end of the story, all the townspeople are very eager to cast their stones, and do not appear to feel one bit of mercy or shame for what they are doing. I found it a very interesting and thought-provoking story. I took a walk at sunset this evening, which was a beautiful sight. As I walked in the cool, refreshing air of twilight, it began to have a relaxing effect on me. The lake reflected the sun's last orange and pink hues, as the roar of rush hour traffic from I-70 added to the regular silence of the park.

## Sunday, October 1, 2000

Nothing much to tell about today. The regular drone of
the Broncos football game on the radio was on for a short
time, until the team began to lose badly. The other typical
sound, that will not be heard after today, was the sound of
the Olympics. Although I love to see some of the events, I
am sincerely happy that they are over. We will no longer
be chained to the television every night and day, and may
even accomplish something! I took a mile long walk today
– the longest distance that I have walked since discharge
from the hospital. It was not comfortable for me, yet it was
not beyond my limits. Although it was a bit trying at the
time, the feeling of having accomplished something above
normal is very rewarding in retrospect. I read an article
by Garrison Keillor today, and found it very interesting.
People do love stories, especially ones about other people.
Some enjoy stories that end happily, and others enjoy
stories that are not, and maybe even wretched. Personally,

I enjoy stories that are not necessarily happy, and in which people must overcome some sort of adversity. The truth is that not one life is completely happy, and all are filled with difficult times and trying experiences; though some may include more of them than others. I enjoy reading literature about real people who have real problems, not fairy tale characters without any real challenges and a happy ending. On the other hand, I do enjoy descriptive writing that makes it easy to visualize the situation or the setting. I appreciate books that transport me into the story, and I can feel what the main character, or my favorite character, is feeling. That is true literature to me. The last thing that I can think of to say for October 1st, is that I can remember exactly where I was a year ago on this date. I was at the opening of the Pepsi Center with a friend, to see Celine Dion in concert. It was so magnificent, with spectacular fireworks and amazing sound. I would not trade that night for anything, as it was so full of excitement.

## Monday, October 2, 2000

It was peacefully quiet about the house today, and I worked on school work and cooked a couple of things. I would have taken a walk, but I was too exhausted. On a happy note, today there were two less pills to take since it is no longer the weekend. Christian came over to visit with us for awhile, on the way to work from his guitar lesson. I did not have to use my inhaler, as my breathing seemed okay today.

## October 3, 2000

I worked on school work for most of the day. This morning, my family and I drove downtown. We stopped by my favorite place, Starbucks, to pick up some coffees to take home. Christian and his family surprised us and stopped by for a visit. My father and I went for a walk in the evening, just before dinner. There are always loons at the lake, although their call cannot be heard above the roar of I-70.

## Wednesday, October 4, 2000

Today was a rather exhausted day for me. I did not feel good, and was very tired the whole day. My mother and I sat in the park a bit to get some fresh air, and a lady with her dog came walking by. She thought that I was a boy because of my baseball cap and lack of hair, as well as thinking that I was allergic to dogs. The latter assumption must have been because of my face mask, and because I avoided the dog when he attempted to approach me and lick me. I am often mistaken and not thought to be a girl, and the only place where I know I can be totally accepted and understood is the oncology clinic at Children's Hospital. My experiences have made me think about all the stereotypes and judgement that our culture supports.

## Thursday, October 5, 2000

Today was a long day at the hospital. I unexpectedly had to receive an IV medicine, that I had once in the hospital, because my immunoglobulin levels were low. It does not seem to be a very pleasant medicine to me. It is called IVIG, and most people react to it. I remember when I had it in the hospital, I had a bad reaction where my temperature spiked to over 104, I had chills, my stomach became upset, and my head hurt. Fortunately, this time I was premedicated and did not have any reaction. We saw a little girl who was in bone marrow transplant at the same time as I was. When I left the unit, she was battling pneumonia, and the prognosis did not sound very hopeful. It was so wonderful to see her at the clinic today! It seems amazing how people can be in such precarious situations, and then be fine the next week. Like my experience in the hospital, when I stopped breathing one day, and a week later I was being discharged from the hospital. That still seems like an amazing thing to me. I was feeling pretty loopy from the Benadryl and Tylenol working together today. The doctor came in to talk about radiation treatments, risks, pulmonary functions, and my lung infection today. It was not a particularly stressful talk, but not a very comfortable one either. I always seem to be at least a little anxious when a doctor is coming in to talk to me. Well, there was not much else to the day beyond the hospital. When there is a five hour IV, it takes up most of the day.

## Friday, October 6, 2000

The weather was a bit drizzly today and quite chilly, but there was no major precipitation. It seemed like late afternoon the entire day, given the dreary gray light. I expect that most of the weekend will be spent inside. I did my normal routine of lots of medicines and school work. My energy level was much improved today, although still not amazing. I was interested to find, in looking at the side effects sheet of my daily IV medicine, that it can cause shortness of breath, or tightness in the chest. The reason that this was particularly catching to me is because I have been having symptoms similar to those of an asthmatic. I cannot imagine how they will sort the side effects of everything out, from the IV medication, lung surgery, lung infection, and chemotherapy effects. I really hope that the chemotherapy is not affecting my lungs, because if it is, I will restart steroids. The steroids could interfere with the lung infection, and make it grow. So, it all seems rather complicated. You win some, you lose some! I watched 20/20 with Barbara Walters tonight, and she had a special with one of Diana's closest workers, who has written a book about the late Princess. It was interesting to hear him speak. Although given to a vow of confidentiality, he decided that he needed to write a book about the real Diana - to demystify her life. She had her own struggles like anyone else, of insecurity, eating disorders, and self-abuse. It seems to me that people do not want to see any flaws in celebrities. It is as if people need someone in their life whom they see as perfect. Someone to look up to who will never forsake their ideals. One has to take the good and the bad with every person though, including their idols.

## October 7, 2000

It was a very cold day in Denver, but there was no precipitation. I felt pretty sick this morning because I did not eat anything that would coat my stomach well enough for the weekend medications. I worked on math for most of the day, as it is my most difficult subject. Late in the afternoon, my parents and I went to do some errands, and then to pick up dinner. There was a bit of a scary experience this evening, as we made a mistake with the flush following my IV medicine. I thought that I had recalled that the heparin reacted with the Ambisome, but fortunately it did not. My experience seemed to be something of a panic attack, as I felt as if I could not breathe, and began to black out. Then after we had called the nurse and learned that they did not react, I began to realize that my "reaction" was just anxiety. Life would not be as interesting without these little excitements!

## October 8, 2000

Today was very calm, as Sundays usually are. I worked on some school work this morning after our Sunday brunch, and then we went to the park. It was a lovely day in the park, with the sun shining, and the reds and golds of the leaves. Many people were fishing in the lake, and it seemed as if the whole world was out in Washington Park. There were joggers, bikers, and other people playing volleyball, soccer, and tennis. It was a wonderful autumn day to be outside.

## October 10, 2000

Today was quite exciting, with another phase of treatment presented. This morning was my first appointment with the radiotherapy doctor, Dr. W. She will be in charge of my radiation treatment, that will be done at University Hospital rather than at Children's. The first thing that Dr. W. did when she came into the room was give me an adorable teddy bear that she said they were giving to all the patients. The teddy bear has a t-shirt with a little poem on the back of it:

*Hug A Bear*
*What's so special about bears that no one should miss?*
*Just give them your hugs and they will grant you your wish.*
*Is it wings you desire to fly over a cloud?*
*Hug a bear, get your wish, you'll make it so proud*
*Is it sweet dreams you need to get through your nights?*
*Hug a bear, get your wish, you will have no more frights!*
*Bears have the biggest, kindest hearts, it's true.*
*Just hug them tightly and make your wishes come true.*

I loved this little poem. After the consultation with the doctor, we were told to return later in the day for the beginning of the planning for the radiation. We came home to the house, and had lunch in the park. I felt somewhat distracted in the two hours before returning to the hospital, and could not concentrate on anything very effectively. When I returned to the hospital, I was taken to a room with a big machine for the planning session. The machine had lasers, that I was told not to look at, and those lasers helped the technicians figure out how to best position me. I had some marks made with permanent marker, that will later become permanent tattoos to pinpoint where the radiation is given. Many measurements were taken with the machine. The other thing that I had done in that room was the making of a facial mask. That was an interesting experience. Each patient has a mask made out of hard plastic netting, that holds the head in place during the treatments. The netting was placed over my face while hot and soft, and took on the form of my profile as it dried and cooled. I was told that I can keep the mask and wear it at Halloween. The last event of the day was the CT scan, to map where my bones are, and to have a general idea of everything so that the radiation can be very accurate. I went into the CT scan room expecting the usual unpleasantness of holding my breath for long periods of time, and was pleasantly surprised. There was one of the new CT machines in the room, and it took five minutes to do the whole scan! I was so amazed, and I was happy to find that I did not even feel claustrophobic. Although it was a bit of an uncomfortable day with the new addition to treatment, and being told new risks, it was not all bad. One thing that I observed is that the adult hospital is quite different from the children's hospital. As soon as I stepped into the facility, I felt a certain drabness and depression in the air. There were no colorful pictures, or any laughter in this hospital. Although the procedures and treatment at Children's cannot be made better, the approach seems to help, as children can still be children there. It seems like the adult hospital would become rather depressing pretty quickly. Although it is depressing to stay in a hospital in the first place, I really do think that the visits from special people, colorful decor, and extra cordial staff help the experience at Children's to be much easier.

## October 11, 2000

I had a clinic appointment at the hospital this morning, that ended up taking a longer time than usual. First, I had my labs drawn, and vitals taken. The bone marrow transplant nurse came in to talk to me for a time, and to verify all my medications. After that, the nurse practitioner came in to see me and do an examination. Then came the dreaded pulmonary functions tests. Fortunately, I was pleasantly surprised by the results of those. My functions have actually improved, which means that I probably do not, and will not, have breathing problems from the chemotherapy. I was very happy to hear that, as it means that I will not be given steroids again to keep my lungs in good condition. When I returned to the clinic to give the results to the doctor, I was surprised by a bunch of people from CU. They were at the children's oncology clinic distributing what they termed "CU Huggies." They are yellow and black pillows in the shape of a huggable person, and they have the CU logo on them. It was very nice of them to do that, and I even met the chancellor of CU! After I was taken back to a room, one of the bone marrow transplant doctors came to see me, and review some issues. Dr. G. was very happy with the pulmonary functions, and he also decided to discontinue one of my daily medications, which makes me very happy. One less pill is always a plus! The other things that we talked about were the pros and cons of radiation treatment, and how the treatment will affect me. Although a lot of the radiation effects sound serious and scary, it seems worth it if the radiation can prevent the possibility of a recurrence. One interesting topic of discussion that came up was my lung infection. I have an aspergillus fungus in my lungs, that would not make people sick, ordinarily. However, since my immune system is suppressed, the infection was able to have a better hold on my system. The aspergillus fungus comes from the dust in Africa, and is actually most prevalent in the sands of the Sahara Desert. This knowledge was a surprise to me, as I usually think of fungus as being associated with dampness. The aspergillus can travel in dust from Africa all the way to the United States. Another thing the doctor told me is that influenza is transferred from Asia to America through tourism, and usually begins on the west coast of the United States, and moves east. So, it was quite an interesting clinic visit, and I learned some interesting facts that I had not known previously.

## October 12, 2000

It was a gorgeous day, and it was so colorful to see the golden and brown colors of the leaves. We took a brisk walk through the park near Charlie's house, and since it was such a lovely day, my parents thought it might be nice to take a picnic to Washington Park. There was a slew of fishermen, sitting in their lawn chairs, and waiting for a catch. Although the fishermen were not too successful, the birds were. There was a great flock of cormorants who appeared to have settled at the lake for awhile. They would dive beneath the water, and surface with a floundering fish in their beaks. Another sight was the Canadian geese, as they would flip completely upside down in the water, which was an amusing sight. I have been thinking a lot about coming home lately. The house in Denver has been nice, but it has never been just like home. On the other hand, I wonder how it will feel to be such a distance away from the hospital when I have been living right in its vicinity for a little over two months.

## October 13, 2000

It was a laborious task to wake up and greet the day this morning. The day was not particularly exciting or eventful. I worked on school work, and replied to some letters that people had sent quite some time ago. Tonight there was a special on 20/20 about the Olympics of 1976, and how the German team was so concentrated on winning gold medals that they doped their athletes so that they would be successful. It is amazing that a country was able to achieve such a dark task merely to win competitions. Apparently, the Germans did intense scientific research, in order to calculate for each athlete when the steroids would no longer be detectable in their system. They tested each athlete before leaving the country for competition to make sure that the steroids were not detectable. The worst part of the scheme was that the athletes had no idea that they were being drugged, and now they are suffering severe effects from all the drugs. Quite a scheme!

## October 15, 2000

As usual, today was Bronco Sunday! I knew that I needed to ask for math help before the game started, so that is what I did this morning. Later in the morning, my father and I took a walk, as usual, and this time my mother joined us. I think that walking is some of the best exercise that a person can get. It is not too strenuous, but it gets the heart rate going. Our walk was surprisingly more exercise than we expected. The park had the sprinkler system on at the time that we were walking, and none of the sprinklers were synchronized with each other. So, we had to run through the sprinklers at different times in an effort not to get soaked. Fortunately, none of us were soaked, and the running gave us a bit of extra exercise. The rest of the day was rather quiet. In the evening, my father and I played boules. Each player is given two balls, and one small ball is thrown out into the playing area. The object is to throw the balls as close to the small ball as possible. Needless to say, we need quite a bit of practice. I do not believe that we will be trying out for the Olympic team any time soon.

## October 16, 2000

This morning, I had to have blood counts checked early, as that is the optimal time for levels. So, that made us get up earlier than usual. When we arrived home, there was a call from the clinic, and everything still looks alright with my counts. My immune system is recovering, and has been for some time since the transplant. The tests that will matter the most to me are the CT scans of my chest next week, to see how the lung infection is doing.

## October 17, 2000

Today was the final planning day for the upcoming radiation treatment. I had some more simulations and x-rays done, and even had some tattoos done! No, not truly. I had three permanent marks put on my chest, where the lasers hit for positioning during treatment times. I had some pictures taken for positioning, and even had the chance to see the actual machine that will administer the treatment. It is a huge structure, and the table that I lay on is not particularly comfortable. It is a cold, metal table, and my neck rests in a plastic cradle that has a bump corresponding with the top of my vertebrae perfectly. There is one consideration for comfort, which is a knee wedge that they place under my legs to keep them comfortably in position. The most unpleasant part of the treatment position is the face mask, that is made out of hard plastic mesh. It pushes into my face, and feels rather claustrophobic. The most frightening discovery for me was the protective doors that close during the time there is radiation exposure. There is not just one door, but five layers of doors, that automatically operate and close very tightly. What feels funny is that there is so much protection for people outside the doors, but the person in the room experiences the full effects of it. It amazed me in the same way that the thought of pumping poison chemotherapy into one's veins does. The drugs are so toxic that even short contact with the skin can burn it away to the bone, and yet the veins and person receiving it can handle it somehow without severe damage. Interesting thoughts to ponder. Christian came to visit today and had lunch with us. My nephew is going to be a rock star with a huge afro for Halloween. His costume is pretty silly! I was thinking about dressing up as a surgeon for Halloween, as the face mask would fit in perfectly. I could have my scrubs, mask and gloves on, with the nametag "Dr. Payne." I even saved the forceps and scissors used from one of my procedures! That would sure scare everyone...

## October 18, 2000

It was an early start today, as it was the day of the first radiation treatment. My appointment was at 9am, so we started out driving at 8:20, due to the rush hour. The radiation clinic was rather full this morning, and it is usually filled with people fifty years or older. This morning there was another young person, a guy about my age. It is always depressing for me to go to that clinic, as all the older people look so ill and sad. I was called back to the treatment room rather soon, and the technicians were finishing up with another patient. I was quite surprised by one of the technicians, who came up to my mother and I and said that she was very sorry, but she had a very bad cold. We were amazed that she had come to work. In consideration of other people, most people would not come to work if they were sick; but to come to work with oncology patients when ill with a bad cold is not acceptable. That simple virus could kill some of the patients, and make the others very ill. The most surprising part was that the technician was not even wearing gloves or a face mask to protect patients. Since my immune system is so compromised at this point, especially towards viruses, we requested that the technician either find a face mask, or someone else. She could not find either, so the other technician alone positioned me, which worked fine. I was very anxious about my first radiation treatment. After all, it feels strange to think that people get a dose of the same stuff that killed people in wars, to make them better. So, when the lights went out and those lead doors closed, I was rather nervous. I heard the machine begin to whir, and then there was a bright flash of light that lasted for about ten seconds. I could have sworn that I felt some warmth during the time that the radiation was hitting my neck, and a strange taste. I became anxious, and believe that I experienced one of my anxiety attacks. I felt as if I could not breathe, and a feeling as if I were blacking out. I imagined the technician coming into the room to find me passed out on the table, but fortunately, that did not happen. Next, the whirring and bright light came again, but from a different angle, and then it was over. One of my concerns with the radiation field that the technician drew on my chest is that my heart is right in the radiation field. Although the doctor told me that my heart would not be in the field, as far as I can see, it is! The doctor says that the field is above my heart. The other thing that concerned me was that I had been told that my lungs and heart would be protected from the radiation, and nothing was put on me to protect them. My hope is that there was some lead protection on the machine somewhere. The other possibility that I have considered is that the machine is so precise, like a gamma knife, that it will focus only on what is to be treated. Both important questions to ask the doctor when I see her tomorrow! After the radiation treatment at University, I went to Children's for my weekly clinic checkup. So, we did a bit of hospital hopping today. My blood counts still look wonderful, and have even increased. I saw one of my favorite doctors, Dr. Q. He took care of me for a good part of my stay in the hospital for bone marrow transplant. Everything looks good physically, and the only thing that I have noticed is that all my fingernails are splitting and peeling off. Apparently this is a normal side effect for bone marrow transplant patients, but more commonly the allogenic patients than the autologous patients. Even so, I was glad to know that it is nothing really strange. I am known about the hospital for having strange reactions and problems that nobody has witnessed before. Finally I fall into the normal category! I have just joined a mailing list online called 4YOUTH, and it is a group composed of young people who are in remission from cancer. Many of them have been through so much, and I have been thinking a lot about that. It seems like some people are plagued with more problems than imaginable, and sometimes it feels like people are being tested to see what their strength is to withstand enormous complications. And most of them pass with flying colors! It is wonderful to have a list full of people who understand everything that I am going/have gone through. Everyone seems to have such wonderful insight into life for being so young, too.

## October 19, 2000

Today was the day of the second radiation treatment at University. The time before the appointment seemed to fly, and before I knew it, the afternoon was here. My father came down to Denver today, as he does on Tuesdays, Thursdays, and weekends, and we all drove to the radiation clinic. It was a long, anxious wait until I was called back to the treatment room. Following treatment, I had my first clinic visit with the radiotherapy doctor to consult on how the treatment is coming. There was not much to say since I have only had two days of treatment. She did most of the talking, and then my mother asked a question about whether the radiation is sufficient enough to cure my cancer, not considering the protocol for the study in which I am a participant. She was on her way out of the door as she was asked this, and stopped to tell us quickly that they had actually decided that I will have an extra week of treatment, that will also be more intense and focused. This was disappointing news for me, and I did not particularly appreciate the surprise manner in which it was presented. Apparently, there is still a swelling in my chest CT scan. There is no way to know if it is cancer cells that survived the transplant, or scar tissue from dead cells. Either way, extra treatment is the safest route because it is better to overtreat than to undertreat.

## October 20, 2000

I had my final radiation treatment of this week today. As my mother and I were waiting in the hall to be called, a surprising happening occurred. I heard chains coming down the hall, and looked up to see two police officers escorting a convict down the hall and into a room. He had ankle chains, wrist chains, and an orange uniform. The other aspect that we noticed was that he was on oxygen, and could not have possibly hurt anyone. It was still creepy for me to think that there was a convict lurking in the area though. Nothing else too exciting happened. I discovered that having the lights on during my radiation treatment greatly aids my tolerance of it. Before it was so scary when the lights went out, the machine sounded its alarm, and a blinding white light would flash on me. With the lights on, I do not feel the bad sensation of the light even though the disturbing sound is still there. The other nicety that helped with treatment today was the fact that my favorite song was playing on the radio as I was experiencing the most difficult part of treatment. That helped take my mind off what was happening. Enjoy the small things in life!

## October 21, 2000

Finally, the weekend! It felt so nice not being obligated to go anywhere for unpleasant procedures today, although I was not able to enjoy the day under the circumstances. Although everyone told me I would not have any side effects from the radiation except for a dry, scratchy throat, I would beg to differ. I felt extremely nauseous today, and was not able to eat very well. It is really hard when that happens because I have to eat something for all my morning pills. My first worry was that my stomach was upset because I had contracted some sort of digestive infection, but then the realization came that it must be the radiation. It is too coincidental to be anything else. Fortunately, by the late afternoon, I began to feel better. I started taking Zofran, the anti-nausea medicine that I had for chemo, and it is even more effective with radiation. So, that helped my stomach troubles, but the fatigue still remained. It is an exhaustion like none other that I have experienced. Even the chemotherapy does not seem to sap energy like radiation. So, I spent most of the day resting and trying to recuperate. We watched one of the funniest movies that I had seen in a while tonight. It was called "Happy Texas," and the premise was that two convicts are mistaken for professional beauty pageant directors, and are commissioned to direct a beauty pageant for little girls in Texas. It is pretty funny!

## October 22, 2000

My stomach was back to normal today, but another problem arose. I began to have chest pains, and tightness when I breathe. This is a new problem, and it had me pretty worried. We called the hospital, and were told that if they became any worse that we should call again. Fortunately, they did not worsen, but breathing problems are one of the most bothersome and worrisome. I tried not to think about the pain or tightness too much. I was pretty exhausted today with no energy again. We watched the third installment of "Oliver Twist" on PBS Masterpiece Theater. It was very well done. I had never actually known the whole story, and had never known it to be so dark. The musical show has a lot of happy music, and that is the only take that I have had on the story. Therefore, I did not think it to be dark, but light and fun. It is definitely not that.

## October 23, 2000

It was back to the radiation clinic today, for the fourth treatment. I felt a little anxious again, somewhat like the first time that I visited there. I am still getting used to being placed on a metal table, and having my head bolted down to the table with a stifling face mask. Before the radiation treatment, I went to the clinic at the hospital, as it seemed that the chest pains had become worse. The doctor examined me and could find nothing amiss, so I was sent down to radiology for a chest film. There was no news of the results from the chest film.

## October 24, 2000

My father came down to Denver today, and he and I took a short walk. I have been feeling back pains, and believe it is from immobility. I was pretty exhausted from the walk, but it was good for me. Christian stopped by for lunch, and then we all had to leave. The radiation treatment went alright, and then there was some extra time between hospitals. So, my parents and I enjoyed some coffee in City Park, and then headed for Children's. Although my CT scan was scheduled for Thursday, the doctor said that he would like to see it sooner than later due to my complaints of pain. The CT scan actually went well, and I was able to hold my breath for the whole interval of thirty seconds. I had quite a panic at one point because the lady came in to ask me when I had my bone marrow transplant. I immediately assumed that she was asking because they had seen something on the scan, and thought that it might be a relapse since the transplant. I was worried, and my father went to ask the lady why she wanted to know. It turned out that she simply wanted to know so that she could see whether or not I had received contrast at the last scan that I had since the transplant. That news brought me so much relief, as I had convinced myself that there was not good news. The rest of the day I relaxed, and recovered from the big day.

## October 25, 2000

It was quite relaxing today, as the only place that I needed to go was the radiation treatment. I have been taking the anti-nausea medicine, and that has made a world of difference in how my stomach tolerates the treatment. I still have chest pains and tightness, and have been awaiting the results of the CT scan. Unfortunately, the hospital did not call today, and I have been wondering and worrying the whole time. I am certain that something will be said tomorrow at my clinic appointment. My inclination is to fear that perhaps this pain is caused by the BCNU, a chemotherapy drug I received while I was in the hospital. On the other hand, my worry has been that the Aspergillus infection in my lungs has gotten out of control, and that it is causing pain again. The third possibility is that the radiation is irritating my lungs more than would be expected, since they have been through so much trauma already with the chemotherapy, surgery, and infection. It is very difficult not to worry about every little pain or abnormality, as it could be the beginning of something serious. I also have difficulty deciding what I need to mention to the doctor, and what is not necessary. I do not want to trouble them with every little concern, and yet it could be detrimental if I do not say anything. After the radiation treatment, my mother and I went to the park and enjoyed the late afternoon there. I intended to study there, but it was so lovely to watch the birds and people that I ended up just sitting. Today was an important milestone in the radiation treatment. It was the end of my first week, so I am one third of the way there. It always feels wonderful to know that I am closer to the end of all this.

## October 26, 2000

Today was the major day of hospital visits. In the morning, I had an appointment at the oncology clinic at Children's. In the afternoon, I had radiation treatment, and then an appointment with Dr. W. The morning appointment at Children's was the one that I was particularly anticipating, since it held the news of my CT scan results. I have still been having chest pains and tightness, and had been sure that the CT scan would hold some revelation as to the cause of the problems. However, we were pleasantly surprised! My CT scan was good, and even improved from the last one that I had. My lung infection is almost gone, the scar tissue from my surgery has healed well, and there was no visible culprit for any pains or tightness. The scan relieved everyone's uppermost concerns, but it is still a mystery as to what might be causing them. They just plan to monitor what happens until a conclusive solution arises. After Children's, my mother and I just had time to come home and have lunch before it was time to drive to University Hospital. I had my radiation treatment, and some x-rays taken. Then I was led to an exam room for the consultation with Dr. W. She did not have much to say. She said that the treatment is going well. She said that I should not feel any side effects, and then she asked me if I was feeling any. I felt that it would be a waste of time to tell her about the fatigue, sore throat, and nausea that I have been experiencing. It has been somewhat frustrating to feel that some people in the medical profession seem to dismiss concerns so easily that patients feel uncomfortable even mentioning them. Even if they are "minor" effects, I feel that it is good to be able to mention them. And people certainly should not be challenged when they are honest about what they are feeling. Just because the general idea is different than what the patient experiences does not mean that the patient is wrong. They cannot control what they are feeling, and each person may react differently than the next. I feel that some doctors need to listen more to the patients and what they actually feel than what is written on their paper. After all, most doctors have not been through it and do not know how it feels.

## Friday, October 27, 2000

Today was a pretty calm day. I actually do not feel the chest pains today. Maybe they are gone! I had my radiation treatment, and then my mother and I spent a short time sitting in the park. Friday is always a good day since it signifies the weekend, which holds no treatments or clinic visits. Just two days of relaxation! This evening, we drove to an art gallery, as my mother has a friend who was holding her first show there. Although I am not allowed to enter any public places, for health concerns, I enjoyed reading in the car. My latest book is "Prodigal Summer" by Barbara Kingsolver. I have only lately begun to read again. It is sometimes difficult after treatment due to fatigue and overall difficulty in concentrating, but I think that it is a good sign that I can read again. It is the beginning of returning back to my regular enjoyments.

## Saturday, October 28, 2000

I did not feel well today. It seems to me that the delayed effects of the radiation treatment accumulate throughout the week, and then all those bad effects reach me by Saturday. I was quite nauseous, and too tired to do anything but lie down today. My whole body ached as if I had the flu. My father came down for the weekend, but unfortunately decided that he should return to Fort Collins. He has come down with a cough and congestion, and the doctor did not tell him anything about what might be happening. It could be a nasty virus or bronchitis, but either way, we decided that it was better to be safe than sorry. I would not have any defenses against an aggressive virus if it attacked my system. My mother and I watched Lawrence Welk on the PBS network, as is tradition for me. It is a really fun show, and provides some good laughs!

## Sunday, October 29, 2000

It was a quiet day today because I did not feel very good at all. I spent most of the day reading and sleeping because I did not have any energy and felt somewhat sick. There was a good movie on the CBS network about a school teacher, and the way that she changed the life of one of her students. In the end of the movie she died, which was pretty predictable. That is how all those movies end! My hair is beginning to come back again. It is in the peach fuzz stage, and everyone loves to touch it, and comment about it. I hope that it never has to fall out again.

## Monday, October 30, 2000

My father still does not sound very good, and unfortunately was not able to come back to Denver tonight as planned. I saw my bone marrow transplant doctor today, and he said that he would like to see my father have at least a week of antibiotics before I am near him. I had a checkup at Children's this morning, and some labs drawn. My throat has been quite sore lately, but fortunately there is no redness or signs of infection. Tonight my mother began to feel as if she was coming down with something, but we are really hoping that it is not the same thing that my father has. Hopefully it is just a passing feeling, and will not turn into anything. My mother and I carved the pumpkins for Halloween tonight. They have rather goofy faces. One is named Fangs and the other is named Nosy. Not scary, but pretty funny in appearance! My mother also purchased a good assortment of Halloween candy. We have Snickers, TasteTations, M&Ms, and Tootsie Rolls!

## Tuesday, October 31, 2000

The thing that we feared has happened. My mother is sick too, so we both have to wear masks around the house for protection. It is pretty scary to think that there is a virus loose in the house, since I am so immunosuppressed at this point. Getting any sort of illness would be bad news. So, I am just avoiding contact with my mother so that I will not catch anything. Christian came over today, but was not able to stay long. My nephew was all revved up for the excitement of tonight. We did not think that any trick-or-treaters were coming at first, but then a whole slew of them came. There was not as much candy left as expected. Hehe… Today was my last radiation treatment with the "mini-mantle" treatment area. Tomorrow I switch to a stronger, more focused beam of radiation. It will not be diffused at all. At least it will not be hitting my esophagus, which may be the cause of the really sore throat.

## Wednesday, November 1, 2000

My mother moved to the basement of the house today, so that we would be even further apart. Her cold has gotten worse, and this setup will ensure even more that I will not get it. Unfortunately, my throat is very sore, and has been for awhile. It is something to monitor since it might be the beginning of a virus. Today began my more intense radiation treatment. It was not a very pleasant visit to the hospital today. I needed to have new measurements and x-rays done since the area they will be treating now is very small and focused. After over an hour on the table, and about five or six x-rays, I was ready to begin the new treatment. I was very uncomfortable when I was finally able to get off the table because my head had been in the mask the whole time, and was bent back into a stiff position. At least the technicians told me that even though it was such a long time today, it will mean a shorter time for positioning from now on. My father came down to Denver this afternoon right after his class in Fort Collins since it is pretty difficult with my mother sick, and my not being able to help her. He has canceled his Friday class and will stay until Sunday night.

## Thursday, November 2, 2000

I had a very long day today. My father and I left the house around 7:30am to be at the oncology clinic by 8am. It was amazingly empty. There was only one other patient there, and most of the employees were not even there. I was taken back to the infusion room, and we discovered that they did not have my medicine ready yet because they were expecting me an hour later. Fortunately it worked out because I needed premedication anyway. I had IV Benadryl and Tylenol to counteract the bad effects of IV immunoglobulin, and then the medicine was started. I took my good book to read, but instead ended up sleeping for most of the time. I suppose that it was the combination of the Benadryl and the extreme fatigue that I have been experiencing lately. The medicine finished surprisingly late. I had been expecting to be finished by 12:45pm, and to have plenty of time to reach University Hospital – perhaps even some extra time. Instead, I finished around 2pm, and it was a bit of a rush to get to the other hospital in time. Everything worked out fine though. The technicians forgot to turn the lights on during the treatment, so I was a bit more anxious. I have noticed that the treatment this time is longer than the one last time. It seems to be about thirty seconds from one angle, and twenty from another. After the treatment, as usual on Thursdays, I was escorted to an exam room for the weekly consultation with the doctor. Dr. W. was gone at a conference, so I met another doctor. He was very cordial, and much more likable. He did not stay for long. I have had a very sore throat, and he was the third person to look at it today, and say that there is nothing to see. It seems hard to believe that because it is almost too painful to swallow! He said that if it begins to bother me too much they can prescribe a Tylenol with codeine elixir. On second thought, he suggested regular Tylenol elixir, and that seemed to help me a bit tonight. The other exciting event of the day that I forgot to mention was the nasal wash that I had done at the clinic. Since both my parents are sick, and nobody can see anything in my throat, they decided to do a nasal wash to see if there is a virus lurking or developing. It was rather unpleasant. The nurse hooked up a tube to suction, and then squirted saline inside my nose. Then she proceeded to stick the tube way up in the membrane, and suck out anything she could find. It hurt and really made my eyes water. Another experience to add to my list!

## Friday, November 3, 2000

Today was a pretty quiet day. The biggest event that happened was going to my radiation treatment. Not very eventful, thank goodness! I finished my book, "Prodigal Summer" today, and will start a new one tomorrow. My mother is still not feeling well, so continues to live downstairs. It is fun to play "nurse" for her, and prepare the meals. My appetite has been really bad lately because I always feel sick. I am certain that this new, more intense radiation treatment is a lot harder on me. The doctor told me that about a week after radiation therapy is over, I should begin to feel better. She said that I can go home after my last treatment next Tuesday! I have certainly been anticipating that day for a long time, and feel that going home will help me a lot, mentally and physically. It is good to be in the familiar surroundings, and it will be good not having to think about going to at least one hospital every day.

## Saturday, November 4, 2000

My mother woke up this morning, and said that she felt perfectly fine, so that was good news. Unfortunately, I felt as if my condition had gone from bad to worse. My stomach was completely out of sorts, and I did not feel well overall. By the afternoon, I was not feeling any better, but went on a car ride with my parents to do some errands downtown. I cannot wait until I am able to go places again. Sometimes it becomes rather dull spending all my time in the house or in the car. The only places I can go are hospitals. I watched the Radio City Music Awards tonight, and that was an interesting program to see. Although I do not appreciate much of the music that is popular, it was fun to watch. They had one award that was for the most influential person who has shaped the music of many performers today. I assumed that it would be someone classic like Jerry Lee Lewis. They said that it was David Bowie last year. Instead, it was a person that has produced a bunch of rap albums! Anyway, it was interesting to watch.

## Sunday, November 5, 2000

I did not feel much better today than yesterday, and spent most of my day resting in bed. Fortunately, by the afternoon, I finally decided to take the anti-nausea medicine, which improved my situation greatly, at least as far as nausea was concerned. Unfortunately, there is nothing that can help my fatigue, and even sleeping a lot does not cure this kind of tiredness. I felt somewhat anxious tonight because my chest felt tight, and I felt incredibly dizzy. I decided to try the inhaler again, and although it has not helped me much in the past, surprisingly, it did help me and I felt much better tonight than other nights as far as respiratory comfort is concerned. My father returned home to Fort Collins tonight. I watched the "Saturday Night Live Presidential Special," which was pretty funny. This morning, to satisfy my curiosity, I went online to research the secrets of Narcan – the medicine that reverses narcotics. It reversed the effects of my morphine while I was in the hospital. I learned that the drug has the possible side effect of causing cardiac arrest when given post-operative, which is when I received it. That solved the mystery of why there was a defibrillator in the room during the commotion. I am very glad that I did not experience that side effect!

## Monday, November 6, 2000

Today was a complete schedule with a little bit of everything. I went to the clinic this morning for blood counts and levels, and then proceeded on to pulmonary functions tests. As usual, it was quite exhausting to inhale, exhale, and hold my breath a lot, but the work was worth it! My tests were slightly better as compared to the past time, which was wonderful news. My counts are still acceptable, but the doctor told me that he cannot promise they will remain there. My physical checkup was very good, although there is a bit of concern regarding my kidneys. The creatinine level has increased, which signifies that the IV medicine that I take for the lung infection is disturbing them. That medicine has been decreased to twice a week now, and I am told to consume more liquids every day to keep my kidneys functioning. Up until this point, I had assumed that a higher creatinine level would mean better function, but now I expect it means a toxicity. I need to be careful. I had an EKG and an echocardiogram today, which were both good. It was interesting to see that my broviac, even though it is on the right side of my chest, goes across my chest and into my heart. Although I already knew this, it was amazing to actually see it. It is always exciting just in itself to see my heart muscle pumping on the screen. It almost makes the discomfort of positioning worth it. Other than all my tests at the clinic, I had my next to last radiation treatment, which went very well.

## Tuesday, November 7, 2000

Election Day! That fact did not mean anything to me yet this year, but next time it will! I woke up not feeling very well today, and seemed incredibly tired. However, that has seemed to be the case ever since the beginning of radiation treatment. It was some comfort knowing that today was my last day though!! Christian came to visit in the afternoon, and then I embarked on the last trip to University Hospital for treatment. The treatment went well, as usual, and then it was over! I had a final consultation with my doctor to wrap everything up, and she had some surprises for me. One was a certificate saying that I had completed radiation treatment, and it is signed by Dr. W. That will be a nice memento. The other was a necklace that has beads spelling out my name, and also six other special beads. There is a program that has started at Children's, and has apparently spread to University, that enables patients to acquire certain beads for certain procedures, treatments, and experiences. The idea is that when patients wear their necklaces, and other patients see them, then they will know what that particular person has experienced. If it is something that the other person will be experiencing, then they can ask that person what it is like. Mainly, it serves the purpose of a souvenir though. I have not begun my necklace yet, but it is certainly off to a good start with the radiation beads! The other souvenir that I have from my radiation treatment is the plastic face mask that was bolted down to the table, to hold me in place for treatment every day. It is definitely unique to have a plastic mold of my profile. I suppose that not many people can say that they have a mold of their face. The other news is that there were two more convicts in the radiation clinic today, chains and all. They had a policeman guarding them, as the other convict had, but these ones did not look as ill. I even made eye contact with one of them inadvertently. Every time I see one, I wonder to myself what they might have done to serve time. Somehow it is comforting to know that cancer affects people equally who do not lead good lives, or hurt others, as well as people that try to be good. That reasoning does not sound very wonderful. Anyway, I left the hospital today in high spirits, and with a great sense of relief. It feels so wonderful to have completed the treatment! Although the last treatment was over twice as long than this one, this one was by far more difficult. Next comes the good part, when I can begin to feel well again, and return to everything that I enjoy!

## Wednesday, November 8, 2000

I have completed radiation treatment, and I am very happy to be writing this journal from my own bedroom! I've been in Denver since August, so it is wonderful to be home again. Walking through the door tonight was the happiest homecoming I have ever had. My father was here to greet us with dinner and hugs, and there were flowers and balloons with cards from friends waiting for me. It was so moving to realize that I had made it home, tears came to everyone's eyes. I know that I will never take being able to come home for granted again, and it felt like returning from a war. In essence, it is a war. Cancer is the enemy, and we are fighting against it. Armed with the weapons of chemo and radiation, we go into battle – and we have won. I received a book in the mail tonight that is a compilation of questions answered by teenagers who are survivors. They share stories of diagnosis, dealing with changes, difficult choices, and surgeries. But through it all – they were able to survive, and come out with a positive outlook on life. One of them states – "I have lived through something that many others have never experienced. Those who have experienced it, and are living with it now – more power to you, because you are the people who know what this world is all about." I feel that perhaps coming home was especially meaningful to me this time, as I was not sure when I left in August that I would ever be returning again. When I look back on the whole experience, and my treatment last time, I do not regret that any of it happened. If I could change anything in my life, it would not be the cancer.

## Thursday, November 9, 2000

It was wonderful to sleep in my own bed last night. It is amazing what an improvement such a small difference can make! Today was basically a day of settling back into the house. We did a great deal of unpacking, and rearranging of everything. It was so great to be back in my own room that I was inspired to clean it! That is not a regular occurrence for me. Later in the afternoon, we felt like getting out of the house for a bit, although it was quite cold. We drove downtown, and walked around for a short time. While my mother went into a store, my father and I went window-shopping. There was one store that had figurine ornaments with guns, which hardly seems like the spirit of Christmas. It seems amazing to me that the holidays are practically here already.

## Friday, November 10, 2000

I began to work a little bit again today. I can already sense a difference in my energy level, and the way that I feel, since radiation treatment ended. I feel much less exhausted and no longer have nausea, except for the weekends. I wrote a few "thank you" notes, and that is about all. Now that I am not going to the hospital for treatments, it seems as if not much happens.

## Saturday, November 11, 2000

Today was a rather quiet day. We watched an interesting movie tonight. It was called "Bicentennial Man" with Robin Williams. It is an intriguing movie that looks into the future, where families have robots as members, and artificial organs can be made, so that people live forever. I thought about how wonderful it would be if people could have artificial organs and bodies, so that they would never get sick or have problems.

## Sunday, November 12, 2000

My accompanist came for breakfast, and to visit this morning. My hands are still too weak to play the cello, but perhaps by next week. She and my parents talked a lot, and then we came to the subject of therapy. I have felt that it would be helpful for me to be able to talk to someone. So, we talked for awhile about therapy and medication. It was interesting to hear what she had to say, since her perspective is different, being in the profession. After she left, my mother and I quickly got packed and ready, to drive down to Denver again. We thought that it would be a good idea to be in the city the day before my appointment in case the weather should be bad tomorrow. My mother did some cleaning, and I worked on some school work.

## Monday, November 13, 2000

Today was my weekly clinic appointment, and everything went well. My health has been fine. It was the insurance company that caused the concerns today! Regardless of what the people at the clinic said to the insurance, they would not pay for a necessary medication. So, it was quite awhile before we even saw anyone. The appointment was at 10:30, and we did not see anyone until 12:30! That was okay though. I was able to visit with a lot of people that I wanted to see today. I went up to the fifth floor after my clinic appointment, and visited with some nurses that have taken care of me in the past. It was so wonderful to see everyone again! I think that it was wonderful for them to see me looking healthy too. My friend told me that she notices a startling difference in my appearance now, as compared to the way that I looked when she saw me in the hospital. I saw the activity lady who makes sure all the patients have something fun to do while they are in the hospital. She gave me the book where the nurses record the condition of each patient, and told me to write something to the nurses in it. She said that they would be thrilled when they read it. I got to see the nurse who handled my transplant, and also one of my night nurses. It is amazing – the bone marrow transplant unit is completely empty now – so no nurses were in there. What is really sad is that six people are being admitted on December 1, which means that they will definitely be there for Christmas and New Years. I am determined to do something for them because I cannot imagine what it would be like to be in there during holidays. It is bad enough without the added grief of missing the happiest time of year. After I had visited upstairs, I returned to the oncology clinic on the fourth floor, and saw my social worker. She was really happy to hear that I had come home, and that everything was going so well. I also saw the little two year old girl who was in the bone marrow transplant unit during the time that I was there. She has leukemia, and it was her second transplant. Her father said that the leukemia has already relapsed. I am so sad to hear their news. It does not seem at all fair that babies and toddlers get cancer. They have not even had the chance to live the simplest years of life. Cancer really makes one grow up quickly, so it seems as if those children will never be able to enjoy just being children. I so wish that I could help them in some way! All this while that I had been visiting everywhere, it was actually to pass time while I waited for another medicine to be ready. It was still not there, so I went to visit the other social worker, who took my case during last treatment. She was very happy to see me doing well too. We talked for a time, and then returned to the clinic, to find that the medicine had been delivered! So, we went home around 3:30. Needless to say, we had quite a late start on the trip home because we also had to do some more picking up around Charlie's house, and pack more to bring home. We got home in plenty of time though.

## Tuesday, November 14, 2000

It was a rather quiet day today, and I was able to relax, and return to some school work again. This morning, I made the fateful call to the therapist, and met with her answering machine. I waited for the return call all day, and finally gave up. Tonight, however, the telephone rang, and it was the therapist! She discussed scheduling, considerations, and a few other things with me. I was afraid that she might ask something like "what did I want to get out of therapy" which would have been a very difficult question to answer on the spot. She simply wanted to become a little acquainted before the first appointment, which seemed like a good idea. It broke the ice over the phone, which must be the most difficult part of a new relationship in person. I am hoping that therapy will be a good thing for me.

## Wednesday, November 15, 2000

Today was work, work, work! I have really been trying to catch up in all the classes where I have fallen so far behind. Some things that I have severely neglected had fallen by the wayside, and I needed to rescue them. I did not do much else today. One thing that has really helped me to concentrate on my work, even in the evening, is that the television is not working right now. I do not even miss it really. I hardly watch anything anyway, and it is just an easy distraction. Reading is much better.

## Monday, November 20, 2000

Today I had an appointment at the oncology clinic. The wait this time was not nearly as long as last time. As I was waiting for my doctor, another doctor came into the exam room. He was from endocrinology, and told me he had gotten permission from my BMT doctor to come and see me about a study. The hospital is conducting a study of the "Incidence of Osteoporosis in Bone Marrow Transplant Patients." I have been invited to participate in the study, which includes an x-ray of the hand called a bone age, a DEXA scan that is a scan of the bones, and a physical exam. I am not quite sure whether or not I would like to participate at this point, but I have a few weeks to decide. It is unnecessary radiation exposure, which is something

I would be in favor of avoiding at this point, since it presents more of a risk for leukemia. However, I would be somewhat interested to see if I have any osteoporosis, and the bone age would tell me if I will grow any more. My doctor came in a while later, and did my physical exam, and everything still looks good. I am on day +86 today, so I am nearing day +100, when there will be a re-evaluation of everything. The best news that came out of the clinic visit is that I do not have to go back to the hospital until next Wednesday, rather than next Monday. Two extra days without the hospital is always good. One subject that the doctor brought up was that my estrogen level is rather low. That is the reason that I have been having some hot flashes. They have not decided whether they are going to do anything about it yet.

## Thursday, November 23, 2000

I woke up early this morning because I thought that the Macy's Thanksgiving Day Parade would be on at 7am. It turned out that it was not airing until 9! It was alright though. I pretty much relaxed all day and accomplished nothing. I surfed the web, and then watched the parade. After that, I watched a little bit of "It's A Wonderful Life." This is the first year that I have not contributed anything to Thanksgiving dinner. I did a lot of surfing on the internet because that is how I am purchasing my Christmas gifts this year, since I cannot go into stores. It was a wonderful Thanksgiving! It was just my parents and I this year, so it was quiet, and I like it that way. I know that I have a great deal to be thankful for too!

## Saturday, November 25, 2000

I did not feel well at all today. My stomach was very upset, and I just was not feeling great overall. It felt as if I had some kind of flu. Due to my physical condition, I was not able to do much of anything, so I just lay around the house. We watched "Chicken Run" tonight, and that was very cute.

## Sunday, November 26, 2000

I felt much better today, but there was a new concern. I began to have shooting pains up my left side. I was worried that something seriously wrong may be happening, like the lung infection returning, or a heart problem. We did not call the hospital because I did not have a temperature, which is usually the case with an infection. We decided that we would wait until tomorrow to see what happens. I did some school work today, but not too much. We watched "The Santa Clause" on television, and that was pretty funny.

## Monday, November 27, 2000

The shooting pains were subsiding this morning, and I came to the realization of what must have caused them. I did some exercise, including sit-ups a couple days ago, and must have irritated something. Also, the pains were on the side where my lung surgery was, which would probably be more easily irritated than usual. So, the problem is solved, and the pains are fortunately nothing medical. Since I felt better, I was able to get more done today. I forgot to tell the most exciting news about Sunday. My parents gave me an early Christmas present – a treadmill! It is wonderful. It is manual, and quite small, so it does not take up much space. Now I can exercise without going outside in the cold weather, which seems to irritate my lungs a lot.

## Tuesday, November 28, 2000

Today was not too exciting. My mother and I ordered a bunch of Christmas gifts online this morning. I did some school work, and my father and I took a walk to the lake, to feed the geese a bunch of old hot dog buns. They certainly enjoyed them! Other than that, I just watched "Frasier" and "Once and Again." I have decided not to participate in the study of osteoporosis in bone marrow transplant patients. It is extra unnecessary tests, and more time spent at the hospital that I would rather not have, along with the extra radiation.

## Wednesday, November 29, 2000

My clinic appointment was this morning, and as usual it made me pretty anxious. I worsened the feeling by forgetting to request a decaffeinated beverage at Starbucks, so the whole morning I was completely wired and on the edge. My checkup went well, and everything checks out physically. The only concern was the pains that I have been having up my side. The doctor wanted to ensure that it had nothing to do with my lung infection, so I had a chest x-ray taken, and everything turned out fine.

## Thursday, November 30, 2000

Today was the much anticipated first appointment with the therapist. I was quite nervous prior to the appointment, wondering what she would be like, and how she would go about everything. When my mother and I entered the house where her office is located, she was waiting there for me. She said "Danielle?" I said yes, and then my feet froze to the floor, and I could not get through the front door because I was nervous. Fortunately, since my mother was behind me, I was able to move on, and approach her. She introduced herself, and then we proceeded up the stairs to her office in the old house. It was very comfortable, with softly cushioned chairs, and a huge, comfortable vinyl couch. I was very tense! My mother was seated a short distance from me, the therapist was across from me, and I was able to have a good view of both of them. I wondered if there was some science in the way that we were seated. Anyway, today was mostly an introduction day, and nothing other than a bunch of questions and answers were exchanged. I had to think back to before any illness, and then back to the first time I was diagnosed, and the first treatment. It was a pretty intense mind practice for me because I have forgotten much of what happened, since so much has occurred since that time. The therapist is very nice, and I like her soothing voice. It makes me feel more at ease when someone has a calmer voice. The rest of the day was pretty normal after that. My mother and I went to the grocery store, and then we went home. I did school work, and before I knew it, it was time for bed. I stayed up pretty late tonight, writing in the other journal.

*Life*

*Have a happy joy ride –*
*Enjoy it while it lasts.*
*Always be the most positive,*
*And forget about the past.*
*Imagine you will be dead,*
*Before the coming of each tomorrow.*
*Make the most of what there is,*
*So there is not any sorrow.*

It has been a long time since I have written in here. I am feeling very scared lately. Not because anything is wrong, but since there is so much that could go wrong. I had my first therapy appointment today, and it made me seriously think about my first treatment. It almost seems like I am doomed to be sick for the rest of my life. Sometimes it feels like life is not worth living with this cloud of worry over everything. Think of one word to describe how I feel right now? Depressed, hopeless, LOST? It is so hard to put emotions into words – that's why I do other things. Well, everything looks worse when I am tired...

## Friday, December 1, 2000

I cannot believe that it is already December! It seems as if the month came much too quickly, and I have not had nearly enough time to prepare for the festivities. Today was not too exciting. I completed some much needed correspondence this morning, and then rested in the afternoon. I did some homework, but it was difficult for me to concentrate. I seem to have lapses where it is challenging to read and/or write. I guess it is thinking about everything that is happening, and has happened. We ate dinner pretty late tonight, and now I think I will write in my other journal.

I feel that talking at therapy yesterday made me think about a lot of things that I might have not pondered otherwise. I do not see that as a bad thing because I feel that a lot of things have built up since my first treatment. I just kept keeping everything inside and to myself, and now it is all cascading down on me. And this last treatment with the scarier experiences seemed in a sense like the last straw. I have had it, and I feel really crazy and bad most of the time.

## Monday, December 4, 2000

Today marks exactly one hundred days from the day of my transplant, which means that the most critical time period following transplant is over. I still must be careful, but am no longer as much at risk for infections and complications. The one hundred days also signifies the time for re-assessment, to ensure that the cancer is completely in remission, and in my case, to see that the infection in my lung is improving. The first thing that I was scheduled for this morning was pulmonary functions tests, which I abhor. Fortunately, everything went alright, I did not pass out in the process, and the test results are even more improved than the last time. That is very good news. The next stop was back to the oncology clinic to see the doctor, have blood counts, and have my examination. There were a lot of tests done with labs. The doctor said that everything looks very good, and that I look healthier every time that he sees me. He considers me about 80% recovered from my transplant. The best part is that he discontinued some of my medications. Today, he cut out Nystatin, Troche, Peridex, and Amphotericin. It is nice to be done with those drugs, but what I really want to stop is the potassium supplement and Septra! Oh well, I have to take what I can get, and the Nystatin does take my daily pill consumption down by eight pills, which is always good. I am expected to be on Septra (the one that makes me feel so sick on the weekends) for a long time – at least until next summer. After the doctor's consultation, there was not as much time as we had expected between that and the next appointment. So, my mother just went downstairs to get us a snack, and then I had my cardiology appointment. First I had the EKG, which was quick, and then the echocardiogram. I watched "Mission Impossible" during the echocardiogram, and it was very nice because the person who was doing it this time did not jab me as hard in the ribs as everyone has before. That made it not such an unpleasant experience. After the echocardiogram, I was finished for the day! Although it does not seem like I did much, the day was pretty exhausting for me. At least all of the tests turned out well. I had a big dinner tonight, since I know I will be NPO (no food or liquid) for a while tomorrow.

Here the holidays are coming, and I feel the lowest I have felt in my life. I am so scared!! Today we saw the two year old girl I knew from the bone marrow transplant unit at the clinic with her father, and it sounded like they might not do any more for treatment. She might be dying, and I feel more upset than words can say about that possibility, and I cannot do a damn thing about it. The doctor told me today that every time he sees me, I look healthier. It seems ironic because every time I see them, I feel like I have gotten even more screwed up emotionally. I should be feeling better, since all this is coming to an end, but instead I feel worse. I am supposed to be very happy, but instead I am so depressed I may as well be dead. I do not know what is so screwed up about me, but I guess I cannot help the way I feel. Today was the first of three days of workup to assess that the cancer is gone. I had EKG, Echo, and pulmonary. Everything looked good, but I do not feel happy about it. Coming off treatment is so hard, especially after being deceived twice. There is no more reason to think that I will be cured this time. The thought of that little girl, and the odds that only sixteen people in the country have had her cancer, made me think back to my treatment, when they told me only six had had mine. A scary thought for me. I cannot keep living with worry. I must do something.

## Against the Flow

*Explain the pain that is felt inside –*
*A deadness that will not cease.*
*Needing to feel alive,*
*And yet wishing to be dead.*
*Not knowing why*
*These feelings are at hand.*
*Moving with the current,*
*Yet reversing the flow.*

*The rock that burdens others,*
*In the current of life.*
*The grand boulder of the river,*
*That serves no other purpose,*
*Other than to deter the current*
*Every so often.*
*The ugliness of the river –*
*The obstruction,*
*Of a smooth, beautiful current –*
*Made imperfect.*

## Tuesday, December 5, 2000

All the tests scheduled for today were my least favorite. I had a bone scan, and a few CT scans. The first thing that happened was the bone scan injection of Technetium, that is given two hours before the scan itself. Then, there was about an hour of waiting, during which I saw my social worker, and visited staff on the inpatient oncology ward. It was nice to talk with everyone again, and it passed the time. At 1pm, I returned to radiology to get my delicious contrast, which was lemon flavored this time. Some people say it tastes like lemonade, which is not at all close to the flavor; others say it is like Kool-Aid, which could not be right even in the wildest of dreams! The contrast just about made me sick, but I was able to keep it down. It tasted like lemon meringue pie that had gone bad. I had the bone scan around 1:45, and after that was done, at 2:20, I was escorted down to CT. The CT scan took a surprisingly short time – only about half an hour. I had my chest and abdomen scans done, and as usual, had the long breath hold. I always have to cheat because I cannot hold my breath for thirty seconds yet, but this time I actually made it through the whole time! I learned that the oral contrast, as well as the IV contrast, is a compound of iodine. That was interesting to know because I have always thought that it was barium. I guess that you learn something new every day! I was very hungry, so we ate dinner early. We went downtown to a favorite restaurant, Pint's Pub, and it was the first time that I had been anywhere since being released from the hospital. It was good to get out into "the real world" again, but it also made me anxious. Everything went fine. I am NPO again tomorrow!

## Wednesday, December 6, 2000

My final re-assessment test — the bone marrow aspirate — was done today. The doctor told me that they take a smear of blood from the marrow, as well as a core sample, that is about the size of a piece of pencil lead. I came to the clinic around 12:30, and they hooked me up to fluids and put Emla cream on the site to numb it. I only had to have one side, my right side, done. That was nice because they have always done both sides in the past. I was taken into the room around 1:30pm, and it all happened very quickly. I had Propofol clinic, which always works well for me. Propofol is "the milky medicine" (because it is white), and it was just pushed into my broviac. As the nurse said "Here comes the happy medicine," I started to go under. When I woke up, I thought that they had not done it yet, but the pain in my hip told me that they had. I came to rather quickly, and was able to sit up and drink something. The doctor came back to touch base on a few other issues. My scans were all good, and the lung infection appears to be gone. That means that after tomorrow, I can stop my IV medicine! That is good news because it can cause damage to my kidneys. He also said that they want to arrange a gallium scan, and also another CT scan of my neck. The other issue is that my estrogen level is still very low, which means I may need to start hormone replacement. So, my doctor is going to set up an appointment with the endocrinologist sometime next week. The big news is that I am being returned to the care of my regular oncologist in a few weeks, and leaving the bone marrow transplant program! That is a milestone. Also, I do not have to wear the face mask any more when I go out of the house, which makes it much easier to breathe. I only need to wear it in crowded public places.

## Thursday, December 7, 2000

Today was mostly dedicated to starting school work again, after not being able to work during all my tests. This afternoon, we drove up Rist Canyon to get a Christmas tree. It was very cold up there! I had some anxiety about whether the altitude would bother my lungs, since they are quite sensitive at this point. Fortunately, nothing happened. I made myself think that something was wrong, and had somewhat of an anxiety attack, but once we got into the spirit of looking for a tree, I felt much better. We went to the place that we have gone for the past five years. Unfortunately, they did not have any pre-cut trees, so we took up a saw and cut our own. It turned out that we found the tree right away, and it is just about as perfect as it could be. I did some exercising on the treadmill tonight, so that felt like an accomplishment.

## Friday, December 8, 2000

I worked on school work today, and that was pretty much it. It was a pretty quiet afternoon, and after I had finished my work for the day, I went downstairs to play the cello. I did a couple of exercises, a piece, and then moved on to some Christmas carols. Since nobody was there to accompany me, I decided to accompany myself. I recorded a tape of the carols playing one part, and now I can replay it and play along. It is a lot of fun, and I think that is what I may do for the oncology patients at Children's this year.

## Sunday, December 10, 2000

Christian and his family came to Fort Collins for a special St. Lucia Day breakfast. That was pretty fun. We had the Swedish coffee bread, and the special cardamom cookies that are meant to be served with the breakfast. I did not dress up in the outfit this year, but we still had the Swedish music and food. Somehow it did not seem like it would look right to have a St. Lucia girl with such short hair. It seemed as if the day flew by, and I had not done anything but eat and talk. I was lazy tonight, and I just sacked out in front of the television. I am getting stronger, but am still not completely normal again yet. It started snowing tonight.

## Tuesday, December 12, 2000

I had an earlier start this morning, since there were hospital appointments in Denver. First was the visit to the oncology clinic at Children's. I had a considerable amount of blood taken, and then my exam. First the physician's assistant examined me. Then Dr. G. examined me. Everything still looks good, and my bone marrow tests were free of cancer. They are going to do further genetic testing, as there is a small chance of secondary cancer from all the chemotherapy. My estrogen level is still apparently very low. The doctor wants me to see the endocrinologist soon. I did not realize this, but lower estrogen can cause heart problems, so I certainly do not want that! It is always difficult to consider all these options in treatment. If I do not take the estrogen, I could have heart problems and other problematic factors. With the supplements, there is a chance of stroke. After my appointment at Children's, there was some time until the next appointment, so my parents and I went to a restaurant that we enjoy near the hospital called Café Euphrates. It is Greek food. I just had a quick follow up appointment with my radiation therapist. She wanted to know that everything is going well, and now I only have to see her once a year. That was all the excitement for today.

## Thursday, December 14, 2000

I had my second therapy appointment today, and this time my father came with me. My therapist had him stay in the room about twenty minutes for some questions and discussion together, and then I had time alone with her. It was a heavy session for me, but I truly felt that something had been gained from it, and the weight on my shoulders was a bit lighter for a time after the appointment. My father and I took a brisk walk around the lake today, which felt good. I can now make it all the way around without resting, and do not feel that tired after I have made the circuit. So, that seems like good progress.

## Friday, December 15, 2000

I returned to the hospital today for the gallium scan, and also the CT scan of my neck. The gallium scan turned out well, although the result was a long time in coming. I had the first scan at 1pm, and they saw something in my lower abdomen. So, then they did a second scan. To put it delicately, the darkness seen on these scans can often be waste in the intestines, so that is what everyone expected the darkness was. We waited at the hospital all day, until I was able to try and "change the picture a little." Finally, around 4:30, the picture had not really improved, but they said that it would probably be fine. I guess I did not work hard enough following the advice the lady gave me on Tuesday, when they did the injection (that advice was to eat lots of fiber!). My neck CT was also today. The doctor left a message saying that the gallium scan was negative. We are back home in Fort Collins tonight, and do not return to the hospital until Wednesday.

*Cascading thoughts of fear,*
*Hours of consternation,*
*Waiting in anticipation –*
*Is there a complication?*
*Streaming tears of the night,*

*And broad smiles of the day –*
*Hiding behind a façade,*
*Deceiving in every way.*
*Losing touch with reality –*
*Sinking into the dark,*
*With no place left to go –*
*But the bottom.*
*Going nowhere, but here –*
*Why this sorry state?*
*Wonderment and fear –*
*Of living to this date.*
*Sleepless nights, and troubled days –*
*I'm lost in a deadly, blinding haze.*
*Despair for what can never be changed –*
*Thoughts of a mind, gone deranged.*
*Wait, wait, wait –*
*Maybe there is hope,*
*To save my wretched soul,*
*That can no longer cope.*
*Bring me back to life –*
*This is my last hope.*

I have not been good to myself given the fact that it has been a period of time since I last wrote, but then, what is new about that? All the time I am on the verge of bursting into tears, and I do not know why. What has happened to me? I no longer know myself, and it is as if I have died. I went for a gallium scan and a CT scan today, and both were okay. I am overanalyzing everything too much. I am going crazy. I know it is silly and selfish to feel so depressed, but there is no helping it. What can I do? I feel so lost and scared.

## Sunday, December 17, 2000

I wrapped some of my Christmas gifts this morning, and unfortunately ended up breaking one in the process. Fortunately, I was able to repair it reasonably well, and just hope that the person will not notice. I did some school work today, and otherwise did not accomplish much. It was too windy and cold to go on a walk, so I stayed inside the entire day. I talked to a friend that I have not spoken to for some time. She sounded alright, but is sick with a cold. Her brother has chicken pox! She asked me whether I could come to visit, or get together, which is an absolutely insane notion with my immune system in the state that it is. Some people do not realize how important it is for me to stick by the rules. I am almost ready to begin going out to places again, but it is pretty frustrating because so much stuff is going around now, and that keeps me inside. Hopefully, I will have a flu shot soon, which can protect me when I return to school, and begin going out in public again.

## Wednesday, December 20, 2000

I had my last clinic appointment within the bone marrow transplant program today. It was a pretty long day, but it was not too stressful. I had my checkup, and then an endocrinology appointment. I was prescribed a medicine called Estradiol to relieve my hot spells. I saw just about everyone that I know in the oncology clinic today. I saw my social worker, and also the teacher. I was able to talk with all the people on my bone marrow transplant team, and it seemed like a very happy time. I had my flu shot, so that was a good thing. It seems like such a long time since my bone marrow transplant, but in fact it is only about four months. I feel practically normal these days which is a wonderful feeling. Some of the most wonderful and surprising news for me today was that I have lost seven pounds in a week! I do not know what happened, but something did. I have been eating a healthier diet, and not as much. Perhaps it made a difference, although I would not have expected it to work so soon. I do not have to go for another checkup at the hospital until January 22! Then they will re-evaluate the status of my lung infection, if it is present, and I will return to the care of my regular oncologist. I am excited about this because it seems to be quite a milestone in all of this. To celebrate, we went to dinner at Valentes. That was delicious.

## Wednesday, January 3, 2001

I know this sounds silly, but I am scared of this year. It is the year of my 18th birthday, and I have always had this awful fear that I would die before I was 18. What is wrong with me?! I have had a lot of difficulty sleeping lately, and took Benadryl, Trazodone – anything to help. Last night I took nothing and could not sleep. Go figure. I wish I could just be normal. Most people go to bed, and they go to sleep. I go to bed, and then I start worrying about dying. I have to check 3 or 4 times in all the places for lymph nodes, and then check my pulse. When I fall asleep it is only by accident or exhaustion, and it is a nightmare right before it happens. I do not choose to feel like this. I have no choice. I am going through a phase where I am so afraid of dying, I may as well be dead. I am feeling funny chest sensations that worry me, but hey, I am not dead yet. Well, off to school work. This is something my therapist told me:

**F**ucked-up
**I**nsecure
**N**eurotic
**E**motional
I am fine!!!!!

*Another anxious poem,*
*To try and ease my fear.*
*Until the Benadryl kicks in,*
*I wish I were not here.*
*How good to cry a river,*
*But I cannot shed a tear –*
*The fear is too severe.*
*What will happen next?*
*I already feel so sick.*
*The minutes slowly pass,*
*As I hear the disturbing clock tick.*
*My chest has a peculiar pain –*

*Is it imagined, or is it real?*
*My head is light,*
*I cannot breathe right –*
*I must never be still.*
*The cancer is back –*
*I swear I feel it,*
*And it scares me way too much.*
*Is that a swollen node,*
*Or a vein I feel,*
*Every time I touch?*
*It is probably an imagined fear,*
*But I can never see it as such.*
*Sometimes I pray to live through the night,*
*And sometimes I pray to die.*
*I cannot survive with this fear –*
*And cannot keep living a lie.*
*I hope the night will quickly pass,*
*It gives me too much of a scare.*
*My pulse is weak,*
*I cannot feel it –*
*Is it really there?*
*My mind has gone*
*Into a fearful world,*
*Of night phobic disrepair.*

## Friday, January 5, 2001

Today was just one of those days. I worked hard on school work (math and history). I want to be ready when I return second semester. I am not too far behind. We went to Barnes & Noble to get the "End to Panic" book my therapist suggested. We went to the Chinese restaurant, and my chest was tight even on the way there. I had a massive panic attack. I was dizzy, cold yet soaking my clothes with perspiration, hot, having a difficult time breathing. I felt paralyzed and every muscle in my body was so tense. I really thought I was going to pass out or die. It did not help that people around us were coughing and sniffling. The attack escalated to severe nausea, chest pain, and muscle pain all over. It was everything I could do to choke down a cup of soup. Oh, to feel so fucked up like this…

## Monday, January 8, 2001

Today I had my third appointment with the therapist. We worked on breathing exercises, that I promised to practice this week, and that is a serious commitment! It is pretty silly, but since I could find no paper bag, I used the blue crayon cup to practice my exercises. Oh well, whatever works! Anyway, just thought it would be good to write today. My latest update? I am feeling alright physically, somewhat messed up emotionally and mentally, and becoming a severe insomniac. Otherwise fine.

*Would you know me if you saw into my soul?*
*Is there anything there, or just a deep, black hole?*
*Where is all the truth, and where are all the lies?*
*Everything's a façade – something in disguise.*
*But you can't disguise the feelings, and you can't disguise the pain.*
*You can't hide from yourself,*
*And you wish for a cleansing rain –*
*To wash away the guilt, and hurt,*
*And to feel sane.*

## Friday, January 12, 2001

I feel at a very low point right now. Life in general seems too overwhelming. I cannot get any motivation to work, so I just screw around, and waste time all day. My stress level is sky high although you could not tell from the outside. I am a weak person. I have no idea how I got through treatment. That should have been the hard part, and for some reason the easy part of dealing with normal things gives me more grief. Time to get off my slacking ass and work!

(Later) Obviously today has been somewhat frustrating. I just don't know how to live or function as a rational human being any more. It seems so hard. I am a nervous wreck lately, and every once in awhile the thought hits me that I could relapse again, and they could not cure me. I had an awful nightmare about that last night, and woke up just as I was dying from complications. Having that dream freaks me out so much! I have always thought I would die before I was eighteen for some reason, and I have heard that some people have dreams that predict the future. I am scared to death.

## Wednesday, January 17, 2001

I just feel so fucking upset right now. I am just letting whatever I have in my head flow into my typing hands. I don't fucking care what it may sound like. I have to get this off my chest. I am fucking going insane. Why am I so screwed up? WHY??? I just feel so scared, and confused, and mad, and lost. And nobody is there to catch me when

I am falling. I am falling down into the deepest black hole that exists, and eventually I will hit rock bottom, and then nobody will be able to save me. I just fucking want to scream at the top of my lungs, and get everything out once and for all. Would I feel better then? I guess there is just this voice within me that longs to be heard, but I silence it because I do not feel like it is worth the trouble. I feel such inner turmoil. Sometimes I am not sure that I can go on, and live like this anymore. It breaks my heart, and I can feel my heart breaking because sometimes my chest just aches and aches, and it will not stop aching, and nothing helps it. My soul feels empty and I just wanna die sometimes. What the fuck is wrong with me?!

*Falling*

*Hanging by a thread –*
*Wondering what, or who, may cut it?*
*Entranced by an unknown dread –*
*Hoping someone can save me.*
*Descending faster and faster,*
*Into an unimaginable chasm.*
*There is only darkness –*
*No beginning, and no end.*
*No return from this –*
*Everlasting lonesome journey.*
*No savior to rescue me,*
*From the endless voyage,*
*Into the world of nothingness.*
*Am I living or dead?*
*Sometimes it is difficult to know.*

★★★

*In January of 2001, I returned for spring semester of my junior year. I knew from past experience that I couldn't expect myself to stop thinking about the cancer, and that it would be a shock to reintegrate into high school. I was prepared to feel uncomfortable, for a while, and to be willing to adjust. But just two weeks into the semester, I decided I didn't need to feel uncomfortable, or adjust to an environment that no longer suited me. I was almost an adult in age, and had become one long before in life experience. I decided to stop going to school, and instead pass exams to earn my GED - graduating as valedictorian a couple months later. While most discouraged my decision to become a "high school dropout," and not even take the SAT, my parents fully supported me. In the Fall, I started college as a freshman at Colorado State University. I ended my first year in college on the Dean's List, with a 4.0 GPA in French and psychology.*

## January 23, 2001

Today was my first day back at school! It all felt very surreal. I was so amazed by the number of compliments I received! It was fun and scary at the same time to go to my classes. I have people I know in every class except precalculus. I found out I am going to have broviac out tomorrow.

## February 5, 2001

Am I really going to do it this week? I cannot believe it! I am so scared about stopping school. These days I do not have much feeling. Everything just feels numb, and yet I feel so much. I have always hidden my pain so well, but when I had my blood drawn at the clinic last time, the phlebotomist saw fresh cuts on my arm. She told the doctor, who spoke with me alone about it. Now she knows some of how treatment has affected me. I sometimes wish that I could just obliterate my life after age thirteen. I want to be a carefree child again, but I can never get the last four years of my life back. Last night I just started crying as I was trying to get to sleep. I cried for two hours. I cry a lot lately, and I do not know why. It makes me sad just thinking I am feeling that way so much.

### Ocean of Life

*I am a mere droplet*
*In the grand ocean of life –*
*Not wishing to be noticed,*
*Yet yearning to be seen.*

*A miniscule part of humanity –*
*Easily evaporated.*
*I'm lost as I return –*
*A painful experience.*
*Reclaimed –*
*Drowned in the ocean of life.*

# EPILOGUE

Surviving cancer didn't make me have an eternally positive outlook on life – or wake up every single day grateful to be alive. I suffered from panic attacks, flashbacks, nightmares, and depression. I felt guilty as a perpetual stream of people remarked that I must be so thankful that I survived. They told me what an inspiration I was – for having such a positive attitude – when I had said nothing. I felt like an impostor, accepting undeserved praise, when I didn't contradict them. I didn't want to disappoint them by telling the truth. It felt like a different kind of cancer was attacking me emotionally – just as severely as the lymphoma had attacked me physically; but it felt like there was no treatment for this other invisible illness, and that it couldn't be discussed. I wrote about my depression in a journal a year after treatment ended:

> It is easier to fight when so many people are pulling for you to get better, but mental illness is not the same. People are not pulling for you to get better – if they acknowledge it at all – they want you to snap out of it. They want you to stop wallowing – and decide to be positive and

*happy. It is not wallowing though – it is your own personal hell – and a constant reality. It is not a bad day, or a bad week, by choice. It is unbearable pain that has nowhere to go because it is not acceptable in the same way as physical – or more specifically – visible pain.*

After years of being at odds with the good impression that everyone had of me, in 2009, I was hospitalized for depression, alcoholism, self-harm, and a suicide attempt. The following year – August 26th, 2010 – I celebrated my tenth anniversary in remission from cancer...in rehab. It is not where I had envisioned passing such an important milestone. I felt even more ashamed and weak for struggling with those issues because I was a cancer survivor – and it had been so many years since treatment. Then, in some ways it began to make sense. During treatment, whenever I had any discomfort, there was a drug to ease it; and I tried to sleep through the worst parts. After treatment, I couldn't stop thinking about the people who didn't survive, and wondering why I deserved to live. Realizing that there might be somewhat understandable explanations for how I felt, and my behaviors, did nothing to assuage my shame – but something else did. I received a survey in the mail, inviting me to take part in a study of long-term effects among adult survivors of childhood cancer. It had several questions about physical health – and even more about mental and emotional health – and even substance abuse. When I saw those questions on the final pages of the survey, I considered stopping, and not participating in the study at all; but I decided to answer *all* the questions honestly, and then I nervously sent it. Some weeks later, I received a phone call from a representative, who said she wanted to follow up with me – about some of the responses I had marked on my survey. I panicked, but before I could say anything, she reassured me that I didn't need to worry or feel badly – a significant percentage of respondents said they had experienced mental or emotional health issues after treatment – and she wanted to make sure I was getting the support I needed. I told her I was in therapy, and had been through different inpatient programs – even rehab; but learning I wasn't alone did more to help me than anything I had tried.

It may be difficult to show all the scars after treatment is over – visible and invisible. Once in a therapy group – many years after treatment – I threw out the analogy that surviving cancer had been my "Mount Vesuvius." As the pressure of emotional pain accumulated, my mantle of stoicism began to melt away; and many years later - a long dormant volcano erupted. Treating cancer until it is in remission is putting out the fire - and providing comprehensive care following the end of treatment is putting out the embers. There is a specific need for extensive long-term support because some trauma responses, as a result of being sick at a young age, may not emerge until adulthood – years after treatment. Both patients and survivors must feel comfortable seeking help, if they are struggling emotionally at any point along their journey. Providing information about support resources - especially for latent trauma responses in adult survivors of childhood cancer – is absolutely crucial for care providers who treat this growing population.

# ABOUT THE AUTHOR

Danielle has been a writer for most of her life, and is particularly interested in the literary genres of creative non-fiction and memoir. In *Two-Timed: An Adolescent Cancer Memoir*, she tells her story in an honest and intimate manner – through private journals she wrote as an adolescent throughout her cancer journey. She was diagnosed with Stage IV non-Hodgkin's lymphoma in 1997, less than a month after her fourteenth birthday. After almost a year and a half in remission, her cancer relapsed, and she went through treatment again. She has been in remission for twenty years, following an autologous stem cell transplant in 2000.

Danielle became interested in raising awareness of the potential challenges faced in survivorship. She is an advocate for the creation and implementation of more collaborative support programs to address the unique psychological and emotional needs of long-term adult survivors of childhood cancer.

Danielle went to Colorado State University and graduated with majors in French literature and International Studies. She has lived in Colorado since being adopted from Korea at thirteen months, and is close to her parents, who have always supported her.

Printed in the United States
By Bookmasters